At Issue

Age of Consent

Other Books in the At Issue Series:

At Issue

Age of Consent

Olivia Ferguson and Hayley Mitchell Haugen,
Book Editors

GREENHAVEN PRESS
A part of Gale, Cengage Learning

GALE
CENGAGE Learning™

Detroit • New York • San Francisco • New Haven, Conn • Waterville, Maine • London

Christine Nasso, *Publisher*
Elizabeth Des Chenes, *Managing Editor*

© 2010 Greenhaven Press, a part of Gale, Cengage Learning.

Gale and Greenhaven Press are registered trademarks used herein under license.

For more information, contact:
Greenhaven Press
27500 Drake Rd.
Farmington Hills, MI 48331-3535
Or you can visit our Internet site at gale.cengage.com

For product information and technology assistance, contact us at

Gale Customer Support, 1-800-877-4253
For permission to use material from this text or product, submit all requests online at
www.cengage.com/permissions

Further permissions questions can be emailed to permissionrequest@cengage.com

Articles in Greenhaven Press anthologies are often edited for length to meet page requirements. In addition, original titles of these works are changed to clearly present the main thesis and to explicitly indicate the author's opinion. Every effort is made to ensure that Greenhaven Press accurately reflects the original intent of the authors. Every effort has been made to trace the owners of copyrighted material.

Cover photograph © Images.com/Corbis.

LIBRARY OF CONGRESS CATALOGING-IN-PUBLICATION DATA

Age of consent / Olivia Ferguson and Hayley Mitchell Haugen, book editors.
    p. cm. -- (At issue)
  Includes bibliographical references and index.
  ISBN 978-0-7377-4669-3 (hardcover) -- ISBN 978-0-7377-4670-9 (pbk.)
  1. Age of consent--United States--Juvenile literature. 2. Teenagers--Sexual behavior--United States--Juvenile literature. 3. Minors--United States--Juvenile literature. I. Ferguson, Olivia. II. Haugen, Hayley Mitchell, 1968-
  HQ27.A44 2010
  306.70835--dc22

                                              2009040551

Printed in the United States of America
2 3 4 5 6   15 14 13 12 11

FD186

Contents

Introduction

On May 23, 2007, then Delaware Governor Ruth Ann Minner signed into effect a law requiring anyone younger than eighteen to petition the Family Court for a marriage license, making it the decision of the judge as to whether a marriage would be in the best interest of the minor involved. This law was drafted by Ken Boulden, clerk of the peace for New Castle County in Delaware, who told Women's eNews correspondent Claire Bushey that "the law was broke [sic]. It needed to be fixed." A key component to the new law is that pregnancy no longer excludes a couple from the state's restriction against underage marriage. Boulden explained that the pregnancy provision that once allowed underage marriage was in direct conflict with Delaware's statutory rape law that classified sex with anyone under sixteen a felony, putting the judge in the awkward situation of marrying a couple only to have one of them arrested for statutory rape as they were leaving the court. However, because of the conflicting laws, statutory rape charges in such circumstances were rarely carried out.

Rigel C. Oliveri, associate professor of law at the University of Missouri, explains the history of statutory rape laws, illuminating how certain states have come into conflict with their laws. The laws, originally based on English common law, were intended to make men take responsibility for their actions, regardless of the age of the pregnant woman. Today, however, statutory rape laws are in place to protect children from predatory adults. When they were created, the pregnancy exceptions were complemented by the statutory rape laws, which limited illegitimate births. They were not contradicted as they are now. The only four states left with these conflicting laws are Maryland, Florida, Oklahoma, and Kentucky, with the latter three giving judges the right to grant or refuse a marriage license to a pregnant minor, whether or not she has parental consent. In Maryland, pregnant sixteen- and seventeen-year-olds may marry without a parent's consent.

Pregnancy provisions aside, in the United States the general legal age of consent for marriage is eighteen; however, many states differ concerning parental consent for minors. For example, in Alabama and Utah, a minor can get married as young as fourteen if they have their parents' permission, and if they have been married previously, they do not need parental consent at all. In Virginia and Wisconsin, minors may be married at sixteen with their parent's consent. When traveling outside of the United States, the ages of consent vary widely; for example, in Puerto Rico the age of consent for marriage is as high as twenty-one years old.

Another major issue concerning underage marriage is the high divorce rate. In a survey done by the National Center for Health Statistics' *Vital and Health Statistics*, half of all teenage marriages in the United States end in divorce within fifteen years. Overall, women who get married before the age of twenty-five make-up 64 percent of all divorces nationwide. Another study by *Vital and Health Statistics* shows a direct correlation between teen marriage due to pregnancy and subsequent second births. Early marriage also hinders the education of the teen, with studies performed by the National Survey of Family Growth and the National Longitudinal Youth Survey proving that the rate of unwed mothers returning to school was much higher at 56.4 percent, than that of married teens at 14.9 percent.

In her research for the Center for Law and Social Policy, Naomi Seiler finds that the government, in its attempt to revamp the welfare system, has created incentives for states to encourage marriage and reduce out-of-wedlock pregnancies. The government offers extra funding to states with the highest rate of reduction for out-of-wedlock pregnancies. Seiler argues that instead of focusing on getting these teens to marry, they would be better served by strategies to prevent teen pregnancy, which makes up 80 percent of out-of-wedlock births. Seiler and others maintain that the most logical way to prevent teen pregnancy is to educate teens. The funds allocated to these states would be put to better use, they say, by developing sex education programs to teach teens how to avoid becoming pregnant, rather than encouraging them to marry once they are pregnant.

In defense of the government's welfare reform and marriage initiative, a report filed by the University of Tennessee's College of Business Administration, explains that the government encourages marriage because research has proven that it decreases poverty and improves the well-being of the children involved. The report also makes clear that they actually provide the tools necessary for the couples to decide if marriage is what is best for them, even going so far as to consider marriage education as a work activity. If marriage is chosen, they help the couple find community- and faith-based programs that will help them strengthen the marriage by teaching them communication skills as well as parenting techniques.

Underage marriage is a controversial topic, with strong opinions from both sides. However, it is just one facet of the many issues concerning minors and the legal age of consent. The authors of the viewpoints that follow explore the considerations and complex issues surrounding age of consent.

1

Raising the Age of Consent Would Protect Youth

Dan Jarvis

Dan Jarvis is the research and policy director for the Michigan Family Forum, a private, nonprofit research and education organization.

Even though most people think that teen sex is the result of peer pressure, statistics show an alarming number of girls are having sex with men who are significantly older. This not only results in teen pregnancy, but sexually transmitted diseases as well. Two things that Michigan can do to fight this problem are to enforce stricter laws against criminal sexual behavior and to raise the age of sexual consent to coincide with the legal age for marriage. Teens are not allowed to smoke or gamble until they are eighteen, so they should not have the right to consent to sex until they are legal adults as well. These steps would better protect children and also put sex back into the context of marriage.

Most people who hear about the high rate of teenage sexual activity think it is the result of peer pressure— teenage boys pressuring teenage girls to have sex. While this is a problem, it is increasingly apparent that many teenage girls are having sex with males considerably older, often by 10–20 years.

The Statistics Prove There Is a Problem

To see how much trouble Michigan teens are in, just look at the numbers. The Michigan Department of Community

Dan Jarvis, "Sweet 16: Age of Consent Should Be Raised," Michigan Family Forum (michiganfamilyforum.org), April 1, 2009. Reproduced by permission.

Health estimates that minors accounted for 7,963 pregnancies in 1999, with 37 percent resulting in abortions or miscarriages. Of those minors giving birth, only 40 percent reported the father's age. In 1999, among girls aged 10–14, 54 percent said the father was at least three years older, while 31 percent of those girls aged 15–16 said the father was over 20.

Sexually transmitted diseases are also plaguing our young people. In 1998–99, there were 1,461 new cases of gonorrhea and chlamydia reported among children 10–14 years of age. Teenagers are also one of the fastest growing populations contracting HIV. Health experts believe that most of these children, 90 percent of whom are girls, were infected by older men who engage in sexual intercourse with multiple partners and then transmit the disease to the children.

Solutions to Fight Underage Sex

Saying "no" to predators who are older, manipulative and able to provide financial benefits is hard for adolescents. While teaching refusal skills can help, we must enhance our arsenal of weapons if we hope to curb teen sex.

Michigan can do two things to combat this "predatory sex" problem: strengthen the state's criminal sexual conduct law governing underage sex (commonly referred to as statutory rape), and tie the age of consent for sex to the legal age of marriage.

Minors are simply too young to consent knowledgeably to sex and its potential pitfalls.

While tying the age of consent to that of marriage may seem old-fashioned and contradict much adult behavior, the law can be a teacher and tell young people that our society does not condone promiscuous behavior. More importantly, tying the age of consent to the age of marriage will put sexual intercourse in its proper context rather than establishing an arbitrary age, as if marriage and sexual relations are unrelated.

Currently, the age of consent for sexual intercourse is 16, a younger age than what is required by law for other "adult" behavior. Michigan law prohibits minors under 18 from drinking, smoking, getting tattoos or purchasing lottery tickets, yet sets the age for consent to sex at 16. In short, a minor can consent to sex, they just can't enjoy a good cigarette afterwards.

Stranger yet, minors cannot purchase pornography, but we allow them to consent to sexual intercourse. Furthermore, when their sexual activity does result in an unwanted pregnancy, they must get parental consent to get an abortion. In all, 21 states have an age of consent higher than 16.

Age of consent laws are nothing new. Around for centuries, consent laws make sexual activity with a minor illegal, whether consensual or not. Minors are simply too young to consent knowledgeably to sex and its potential pitfalls.

Even children who are legally emancipated must abide by most laws governing activity based on age, such as tobacco and alcohol use. To achieve emancipation, a minor must demonstrate to a judge that he can manage his own financial, personal and social affairs. All of these elements are also essential to deal with sexual activity and its consequences. Legally, however, our current age of consent law considers all minors over 16 capable of making weighty decisions concerning sex.

Sexual Predators Should Suffer Harsher Punishments

Not only should the age of consent be raised, but stiffer penalties should also be put in place for sexual predators who are significantly older than their minor partners. Our current fourth degree CSC [Criminal Sexual Conduct] law has such a provision. While no law attains 100 percent compliance, all laws have some deterrent effect. The popular term "jailbait" is evidence of widespread knowledge of laws prohibiting taking advantage of minors. It's high time to dust the term off and give it new energy.

Lawmakers should consider amending Michigan's criminal sexual conduct laws to give adolescents more time to reach a point of maturity where they are better able to make informed choices about the consequences of sexual relationships. Our youth and our culture will be healthier financially, socially, emotionally and physically when we protect our children and put sexual activity in its proper context.

2

The Age of Consent Should Be Reconsidered

William Saletan

William Saletan is the national correspondent for Slate, *a general interest, daily magazine on the Web, and the author of* Bearing Right: How Conservatives Won the Abortion War.

When it comes to sex involving minors, the legal ramifications vary depending on the ages of the people involved. The legal age of consent has been adjusted frequently, and many sexually active teenagers are now being categorized as pedophiles, thus doing more harm to these children than protecting them. Children are forced, in today's society, to mature emotionally and mentally at an earlier age, entering pubescence at a younger age than other generations as well. Forty-two percent of sixteen-year-olds score at an average adult level on intellectual ability tests, which supports the age of consent being sixteen. However, emotional maturity also should be considered, and studies show that teens are much slower to reach emotional maturity. Instead of developing ways to regulate teen sex, each age of consent case should be treated differently, with the ages of the parties involved being the first thing considered. More specifically, teenagers should not be punished for exhibiting normal sexual behavior with people their own age.

In Georgia, 21-year-old Genarlow Wilson is serving a mandatory 10-year jail sentence for aggravated child molestation. His crime: When he was 17, he had oral sex with a 15-

William Saletan, "The Mind-Booty Problem: Rethinking the Age of Sexual Consent," Slate.com, September 27, 2007. Reproduced by permission.

year-old girl. In Utah, polygamist leader Warren Jeffs has been convicted as an accomplice to rape for orchestrating a sexually coercive marriage between a 14-year-old girl and her 19-year-old cousin. In Michigan, a 53-year-old prosecutor is in custody on charges of entering the state to have sex with a 5-year-old girl.

This is the reality of sex with minors: The ages of the parties vary widely from case to case. For more than a century, states and countries have been raising and standardizing the legal age of consent. Horny teenagers are being thrown in with pedophiles. The point of this crackdown was to lock up perverts and protect incompetent minors. But the rationales and the numbers don't match up. The age of majority and the age of competence are coming apart. The age of competence is fracturing, and the age of female puberty is declining. It's time to abandon the myth of the "age of consent" and lower the threshold for legal sex.

Onset of Puberty Age Is Declining

The original age of consent, codified in English common law and later adopted by the American colonies, ranged from 10 to 12. In 1885, Britain and the states began raising the age to 16, ostensibly to protect girls' natural innocence. This moral idea was later bolstered by scientific reference to the onset of puberty.

One of every three American ninth graders has had intercourse.

But the age of puberty has been going the other way. Over the past 150 years in the United States and Europe, the average age of menarche—a girl's first period—has fallen two to four months per decade, depending on the country. In 1840, the age was 15.3 years. By the early 1980s, it was 12.8. At first, the trend was driven by nutrition, sanitation, and disease control. Recently, some analysts thought it had stopped. But dietary changes and obesity may be pushing it forward again. Two years ago, researchers reported that the average age of menarche among American girls, which had declined from 12 years and 9 months in the 1960s to 12 years and 6 months in the 1990s, was down to 12 years and 4 months by the beginning of this decade. Among black girls, average menarche was occurring about three weeks after their 12th birthday.

Getting your period doesn't mean having sex right away. But earlier puberty does, on average, mean earlier sex. According to the most recent data from the U.S. government's Youth Risk Behavior Survey, one of every three American ninth graders has had intercourse. And that's not counting the millions of teens who have had oral sex instead.

Puberty Increases Risky Behavior

Having sex at 12 is a bad idea. But if you're pubescent, it might be, in part, *your* bad idea. Conversely, having sex with a 12-year-old, when you're 20, is scummy. But it doesn't necessarily make you the kind of predator who has to be locked up. A guy who goes after 5-year-old girls is deeply pathological. A guy who goes after a womanly body that happens to be 13 years old is failing to regulate a natural attraction. That doesn't excuse him. But it does justify treating him differently.

I'm not saying 12 should be the official age of "consent." Consent implies competence, and 12-year-olds don't really have that. In a forthcoming review of studies, Laurence Steinberg of Temple University observes that at ages 12 to 13, only 11 percent of kids score at an average (50th percentile) adult level on tests of intellectual ability. By ages 14 to 15, the percentage has doubled to 21. By ages 16 to 17, it has doubled again to 42. After that, it levels off.

By that standard, the age of consent should be 16. But competence isn't just cognitive. It's emotional, too. Steinberg reports that on tests of psychosocial maturity, kids are much slower to develop. From ages 10 to 21, only one of every four young people scores at an average adult level. By ages 22 to 25, one in three reaches that level. By ages 26 to 30, it's up to two in three.

Steinberg concludes that "risk-taking increases between childhood and adolescence as a result of changes around the time of puberty in the brain's socio-emotional system." In tests, these tendencies peak from ages 13 to 16. Subsequently, "[r]isk-taking declines between adolescence and adulthood because of changes in the brain's cognitive control system—changes which improve individuals' capacity for self-regulation." The latter kind of competence doesn't reach adult levels until the mid-20s.

Opportunities for Regulating Teen Sex

Lay out these numbers on a timeline, and you have the beginnings of a logical scheme for regulating teen sex. First comes the age at which your brain wants sex and your body signals to others that you're ready for it. Then comes the age of cognitive competence. Then comes the age of emotional competence. Each of these thresholds should affect our expectations, and the expectations should apply to the older party in a relationship as well as to the younger one. The older you get, the higher the standard to which you should be held responsible.

The lowest standard is whether the partner you're targeting is sexually developed as an object. If her body is childlike, you're seriously twisted. But if it's womanly, and you're too young to think straight, maybe we'll cut you some slack.

The next standard is whether your target is intellectually developed as a subject. We're not talking about her body anymore; we're talking about her mind. When you were younger, we cut you slack for thinking only about boobs. But now we expect you to think about whether she's old enough to judge the physical and emotional risks of messing around. The same standards apply, in reverse, if you're a woman.

It's possible that you'll think about these things but fail to restrain yourself. If you're emotionally immature, we'll take that into consideration. But once you cross the third line, the age of self-regulatory competence, we'll throw the book at you.

When you're 35, "she's legal" isn't good enough.

Each Situation Should Be Treated Age Appropriately

What do "cutting slack" and "throwing the book" mean? If you're young, we could let your parents handle it. We could assign a social service agency to check up on you. We could require you to get counseling. We could issue a restraining order. We could put you on probation. We could put you in a juvenile facility, a mental institution, or jail. In the worst case, we could subject you to a mandatory minimum sentence.

Whatever the particulars, the measures taken should be developmentally appropriate. "Age-span" provisions, which currently allow for sex with somebody near your own age, are a good start, but they're not objectively grounded. That's why they differ wildly from state to state. I'd draw the object line at 12, the cognitive line at 16, and the self-regulatory line at 25. I'd lock up anyone who went after a 5-year-old. I'd come down hard on a 38-year-old who married a 15-year-old. And if I ran a college, I'd discipline professors for sleeping with freshmen. When you're 35, "she's legal" isn't good enough.

What I wouldn't do is slap a mandatory sentence on a 17-year-old, even if his nominal girlfriend were 12. I know the idea of sex at that age is hard to stomach. I wish our sexual, cognitive, and emotional maturation converged in a magic moment we could call the age of consent. But they don't.

3

The Appropriate Age for Sex Should be Determined by Individual Maturity

Theodore Dalrymple

Theodore Dalrymple is a prison psychiatrist in Britain, the Dietrich Weissman fellow of the Manhattan Institute, and an author.

Age of consent laws are not being thought of as appropriate for all children, as every child matures, both physically and mentally, at a different rate. Since children reach puberty and mature sexually earlier than previous generations, age of consent laws have had less influence over the sexual activity of many children. Children are deciding for themselves whether their behavior will be harmful to anyone, and, persuading themselves that it won't be, simply disregard the law. Despite these trends, no one makes the argument for lowering the age of consent out of fear of being labeled a pedophile. Parents have not helped, as they are sometimes complicit in their children committing sexual offenses and usually only enforce the law in a situation involving revenge.

If you put "Michael Jackson trial" into an Internet search engine, you get links to approximately 5,110,000 web pages. If you put in "Mao Zedong," you get about 509,000; "Lenin" comes up with 2,770,000. Thus the trial of a show-business celebrity appears to interest the world more than the lives and careers of the two framers of the most disastrous revolutions in world history.

The case is a surpassingly sordid one, of course, and the accused bizarre beyond belief. His celebrity and wealth have allowed him to indulge his whims to such an extent that the most egotistical Roman emperors, by comparison, seem models of psychological stability. And whether innocent or guilty, Michael Jackson is certainly the Nero of kitsch.

That does not mean, however, that the family of his accuser is a model of bourgeois propriety. At the very least, entrusting a minor to the care of a man of Mr. Jackson's reputation would seem a serious error of judgment, and raises questions as to the motives of those who would make such an error. But whatever the eventual outcome of the trial, [Michael Jackson was found not guilty] the case will be of considerable interest to social historians seeking, a hundred years hence, to understand the psyche of the late 20th and early 21st centuries.

Only the sexual behavior of their children is not within the responsibility of parents.

Those future historians (assuming that an interest in the past survives) will be struck, I suspect, by the confusion in our society concerning sexual boundaries. On one hand, almost no sexual display is forbidden, and the most casual of liaisons is perfectly normal; on the other, university professors dare not be alone in a closed room with a female student for fear of accusations of sexual misdemeanor, and in some offices the most mildly flirtatious of remarks is taken as little short of rape. Extreme licentiousness thus coexists with a Puritanism that out-Calvins Calvin. One minute we are told that anything goes, and the next that we must carefully censor ourselves for fear of permanently traumatizing anyone who might overhear supposedly salacious remarks. At last, Herbert Marcuse's concept of repressive tolerance seems to make some sense: We can do what we like so long as we live in fear.

This is not our only confusion about sexual boundaries, of course. Our society is extremely condemnatory of the crimes of which Jackson is accused—he faces a prison sentence of 20 years, far more than he'd get for many other offenses—and yet it sexualizes children earlier and earlier in their lives, with sex education starting almost before they know anything else. Part of this education entails the ethical proposition that no sexual activity between consenting people is wrong or to be condemned, and we bombard children with materials that suggest that a lack of sexual experience by the age of twelve is a failure and a failing; and yet we affect to believe also that premature sexual activity has a permanently adverse effect, being ultimately responsible for all sorts of mal-adaptations and miseries later in life.

In Britain, the only operation on a child under 16 that a parent does not have the right to be consulted or notified about is abortion. Under new legislation, parents can be made responsible for the crimes and misdemeanors of their children, and if the child persistently truants from school, the parents (or, more usually, the single parent) can be sent to prison. Yet a doctor is virtually prohibited from informing the parents if he prescribes oral contraceptives to their daughter when she is 14 years old. Only the sexual behavior of their children is not within the responsibility of parents; and, oddly enough, confidential prescribing of contraceptives has done nothing to reduce the rate of teenage pregnancy in Britain—quite the contrary.

Why Age of Consent Laws Are Broken

At the same time, sexual relations under the age of 16 remain a criminal offense. In other words, British doctors not only do, but must, as a matter of professional principle, conspire in what the law still considers sexual crime. Since it is an undoubted fact, and no doubt part of the problem, that children mature sexually much earlier than they once did—the age of puberty has declined by about a year every decade for several decades—there could, I suppose, be a rational case for reducing the age of consent, but no one makes it for fear of being labeled a pedophile. Instead, parents, like doctors, connive at the commission of sexual offenses. Whenever I have seen men imprisoned for having sexual relations with a girl under the age of consent, I have discovered that, de facto, they are being punished not for having sex with such a girl, but for refusing to continue to have sex with her. She or her parents then (and only then) report to the police, not as a matter of principle but of revenge, the law in such cases being used as nothing but an instrument to obtain a satisfactory end to a lovers' tiff, or what theorists of narrative are inclined to call "closure."

There is, in fact, a deep-seated problem about not only sexual but all behavioral boundaries in modern societies. While most of us who think about such matters at all accept that boundaries are socially desirable or necessary, we also demand that they be rational, that is to say have a justification derived from the very constitution of things. Unfortunately, nature does not often oblige with such boundaries: Continua are more common in nature than discrete breaks.

Each person is left to decide whether his behavior will cause harm to himself or others, and it is a fact of human nature that we can easily persuade ourselves of the harmlessness of what we want, or are already determined, to do.

Children, for example, always have matured and always will mature, both physically and mentally, at different rates. At the age of 15, some will appear all but adult, while others will appear fit for the nursery. What is right and appropriate for one child, therefore, will not appear right and appropriate for another. It is true, nevertheless, that precocity is no longer a merely individual phenomenon, but one that occurs on a social scale: It often seems to me that adolescence is now reached very early in life, but then is never really left. And it is clear that everybody—every parent and, increasingly, every child—expects to define his own boundaries. Few are prepared any longer to accept in practice that a child of a certain age may not indulge in sexual intercourse simply because the law forbids it.

On the contrary, people compare the demands imposed by the legal boundaries with their own particular situation. We all do it to an extent. What driver has not told himself in an area with a 30-mile-an-hour speed limit that a few extra miles an hour won't make any difference, given the road conditions? When the matter in hand is the age of consent, or some other legally prescribed sexual boundary, however, it is hardly surprising that moral chaos results. The question is not whether a rule is right, and therefore must be obeyed, but whether it is right for me, and can therefore be disobeyed. And the only person who can decide the question is, not surprisingly, me. Each person is left to decide whether his behavior will cause harm to himself or others, and it is a fact of human nature that we can easily persuade ourselves of the harmlessness of what we want, or are already determined, to do. And conformity has in any case a bad name: It is a form of lese majeste of the individual, and—ever since the end of the Second World War carries the connotation of the feeble excuse offered by mass murderers, that they were only obeying orders. Not the least damage that Nazism did to the world was to destroy faith in the possibility of decent conventions that ought to be followed.

The Michael Jackson case has revealed a foul swamp of egotism, not just of Jackson alone, though he has hitherto enjoyed the means to live out his tasteless fantasies. The case is an example of what happens when individuals are left to define boundaries for themselves without the assistance of social convention.

4

Age of Consent Laws Are Based on Puritanical Notions

Melissa Kang

Melissa Kang is a lecturer in the Faculty of Medicine at the University of Sydney, Australia, as well as a specialist in adolescent medicine at Sydney's New Children's Hospital.

The concerns about adolescent sexuality are moralistic and stem from Christian beliefs that have prevailed throughout history. Historically, the age of consent was tied into the age at which young women were married and could produce heirs, an economic move made to protect the family fortune and name. Today, however, with studies showing that adolescence is an important time for sexual development, the varying ages of consent do not reflect our current understanding of teenage sexuality. Also, because of puritanical views on underage sex, teenagers are not being educated about safe sex, leading to higher pregnancy and sexually transmitted disease rates. Despite all the scholarly studies, no one has asked the young people themselves what their opinions are, and they should have some say in the laws concerning them. These laws also should nurture the safe development of their sexuality, not punish them for what studies say is normal behavior.

What is the enduring appeal of Romeo and Juliet? Perhaps it is because they were an adolescent couple experiencing the absolute intensity of sexual and romantic attraction to which most people in the human race can relate. While

Melissa Kang, "Age of Consent Laws: Puritan Notions of Right and Wrong," online opinion.com.au, March 21, 2005. Reproduced by permission.

the story is about more than their personal encounters with infatuation and lust, their sexual drives and awakenings—which are central to the plot—are accepted and valued as core human qualities.

Juliet was 14, and about to be married off to the nobleman Paris, when she fell in love with Romeo. Provided she married, sex at her age was OK. Fast forward a few hundred years and adolescent sexuality in Western societies seems a whole lot more complicated, despite the fact that women and men can now control their fertility, fall in love more than once and partner with whomever they choose, and that diverse sexualities are increasingly acknowledged, and in many places, accepted and welcomed.

Concern Is Mostly for Morals, Not Teen Safety

The concerns of some Western societies about adolescent sexuality are predominantly moralistic and a legacy of Christian, particularly puritan, notions of right and wrong. While societies must adopt moral positions on a variety of human behaviours—such as violence, the abuse of children, the exploitation of minority populations—what informs our moral position on adolescent sexuality? Should there be an "age of consent"? And if so, does it serve a moral, or some other, purpose?

Historically, if sexual activity led to pregnancy and childbirth, this created potential complications regarding property and inheritance. Hence, the age of consent was closely related to the age at which marriage and the production of heirs could take place, and served an economic function apart from anything else. The illegality of homosexual sex was (and still is) connected to religious beliefs.

The laws surrounding the age of consent to have sex vary between states and territories in Australia. In some states the age of consent is 16 years for sex, in others the age depends on whether it is heterosexual or homosexual sex, or whether it is anal sex (regardless of the sex of the partner). In most states and territories there is a provision that prohibits adults with "special care" of a young person (such as teachers and stepparents) from having sex with that young person if they are under 18 years. In ACT [Australian Capital Territory] and Victoria, sex between consenting individuals of any sex is allowed between the ages of 10 and 16 provided there is less than 2 years age difference.

Modern theories about adolescence regard it as a crucial period for sexual development.

How well do these laws reflect our current understanding of adolescent sexuality? The law in these latter two states appears to come closest to reflecting the absolute normality of adolescent sexuality, with the age difference provision a reasonable safety check for preventing abuse and exploitation.

Distinguishing Adolescence as a Life Stage Is a Modern Theory

It must be recognised that adolescence as a distinct life stage is very modern: it was only really "invented" 100 years ago. Modern theories about adolescence regard it as a crucial period for sexual development, and, conversely, sexuality is seen as having a central role in adolescent development. Undoubtedly the surge of sex hormones and physiological changes associated with puberty primarily account for these theories, and in studies of human sexual behaviour, puberty appears to be a prerequisite for copulation.

But is it really that simple? When does human sexuality in the individual begin? The human male fetus can experience penile erection and female infants (and probably fetuses) can lubricate. Masturbation and sexual play among infants and young children are common, (although their meaning is interpreted by adults). Childhood sexuality and sexual behaviour have seldom been the subject of scientific or social enquiry.

The cognitive maturity that rapidly develops between about the ages of 11 and 14 is deemed sufficient to enable many young adolescents to consent to their own medical treatment. It is reasonable to assume that the mature adolescent can also make decisions about whether they want to engage in sexual activity.

Adolescent sexuality in Australia has been studied almost exclusively in relation to sexual and associated behaviours. The scientific study of sexuality allows us to identify behavioural and demographic "risk" factors, with the word "risk" replacing the morally-based "wrong". Health "risk" has, in fact, become a thin disguise for an ongoing moral agenda.

Among Australian adolescents, about half have had (hetero) sexual intercourse by the age of 16. The majority of these do not consistently use condoms to prevent sexually transmitted infections and notifications for Chlamydia have steadily increased over the past few years. About a quarter of secondary school students surveyed in the last national sex survey said that their last sexual encounter took place while intoxicated and was unsafe or unwanted as a result.

These scientifically valid findings add plenty of fuel to the fires of both the moralists and the health professionals: they are objective, simple measures of behaviour or behavioural outcomes. In the USA, the alarmingly high teenage pregnancy rate was the rationale for introducing federally funded abstinence-only-until-marriage sex education programs, which required that young people must be taught that "sexual activity outside of marriage is likely to have harmful psychological and physical effects".

Sexual Awareness Is a More Effective Approach

How and why do these "sexual health indicators" justify laws that prohibit consensual sexual activity between two people of any sex? In countries where there is an openness towards addressing sexuality and easier access to health information and services, adolescent pregnancy rates are lower. The World Health Organisation found that across Europe and the UK [United Kingdom], comprehensive programs (including sex education, access to services, youth development, family outreach, and an open and positive attitude towards sexual health and relationships) were more effective in reducing teenage pregnancy rates.

We are still living in the dark ages and it's time that all sexualities are acknowledged and accepted.

A Columbia University study found that sexually transmitted infection rates in the longer term were no different among young people who had taken virginity pledges compared to those who didn't, because they failed to use adequate protection, and that "pledgers" were less likely to use contraception when they lost their virginity.

In the Australian national study of secondary school students, around 10 per cent of males and females reported feeling attracted to people of the same sex, or both sexes, or were unsure. There is absolutely no sense in having a higher age of consent for homosexual sex—is this based on the supposition, or the hope, that in time, young people who are homosexual or bisexual will grow out of it? If so, we are still living in the dark ages and it's time that all sexualities are acknowledged and accepted, with laws designed to protect and promote well-being of all, rather than punishing a completely normal minority.

No One Is Asking the Young People Their Opinions

The voices of young people themselves are also visibly missing in the discussion about adolescent sexuality. What do young people think? What do they worry about? Are their concerns the same as those of adults? Young rural Australian women describe sexual safety as having more to do with protecting their reputations, in a society full of double standards, than with the possibility of pregnancy or STIs [Sexually Transmitted Infections]. Young men and young women cite love, pleasure and curiosity as reasons for having sex.

Young men and women have a diverse range of experiences, questions and concerns when it comes to sex—from how often one can masturbate, to how to negotiate relationships to how to discuss sexual practices with partners.

In a civilized world that acknowledges the rights of the child, young people also need some say in what the law does and does not let them do.

Sexuality Has Evolved Throughout History

Sexuality is a core human quality, and human beings have a vast sexual cultural history. Archaeologist Timothy Taylor argues that humans are unique among the animal kingdom because of the evolution of culture, a development that has taken no less than four million years. He goes on to say that "once culture was invented, cultural variation blossomed" and that ". . . it is possible to document great variation in human sexuality over the past 5,000 years: bestiality, homosexuality, prostitution, transvestism, transsexuality, hormone treatments, sadomasochism, contraception, 'pure breeding', sex as an acrobatic and competitive pastime and as a transcendental spiritual discipline."

At any point in time on any part of the planet, societal norms about sexuality will represent only a snapshot of the way sexuality is constructed at that particular moment.

Romeo and Juliet's tragic fate opened the eyes of the adults in their world, and the play ends with a sense of optimism. In the 21st century, let's make laws that promote the responsible care of children and young people (such as laws that prohibit potential abuses of power for the gratification of adults) and that nurture the safe and healthy development of the individual's sexuality, in all its glorious variety.

5

Innocent Crushes Are Sometimes Distorted

Judith Levine

Judith Levine is the author of Harmful to Minors: The Perils of Protecting Children From Sex, *and she currently writes a column for the Vermont alternative weekly newspaper,* Seven Days.

The way Americans view adult-child relationships has certainly changed since the 1960s, with stricter laws in place to protect children. The author's relationship with a twenty-six-year old camp counselor when she was a fourteen-year-old girl definitely would be considered exploitive by today's standards, even though the two never engaged in sex. The laws in place today criminalize consensual teen sex because society refuses to see teens as sexual beings. In the 1960s a young person's sexuality was considered beautiful, unlike in today's society where it is considered perverse.

This is an innocent story. In 1967, the summer before my 15th birthday, I fell in love. It was my first intense erotic love, and its object was the photography counselor at camp—a lean, bearded, blue-eyed guy I'll call Jake. He was 26. Nothing sexual happened. Still, I think of those two months as the summer of my *épanouissement*, a French word meaning blossoming or opening, which also means glow. Jake took hundreds of pictures of me, and his affirmation and his camera opened me to myself. They helped me begin, sexually, to glow.

Judith Levine, "The Romance a Teenage Camper Couldn't Have Today," *The Village Voice* (villagevoice.com), July 2, 2002. Reproduced with the permission of *The Village Voice*.

Times Have Changed

If the same events had occurred in 2002, they would not be viewed as innocent. The adults around me would write my chaste romance as a perverse tale, casting Jake as a predator and me as his hapless, clueless prey. Had I started my sex education with good-touch-bad-touch lessons in kindergarten or listened for a decade to media reporting on a world allegedly crowded with sexual malefactors sniffing the world for young flesh, I might even have believed that my friend and mentor Jake was one of them. That sweet idyll would have been, instead, the summer of my victimization. And instead of opening me, Jake's attentions might have closed me down in fear and confusion.

A Coming of Age Story

The photographs were another kid's idea. Jake and I and a few other campers were messing around in the dining room after supper early in the summer, and a boy named Ezra suggested I model for Jake. "Judy would make a gas model," he said. *Gas*, in 1967, meant cool. And looking back, I have to say, I was a cool kid. I wrote poetry; I played guitar and piano pretty well. According to the adults who knew me then, I was precocious and perceptive. My friends remember me as witty and impassioned. I affected a late-beatnik-early-hippie look: skimpy tank tops worn without a bra (I didn't need one anyway), low-slung bell-bottoms that revealed the curve of my belly where it dipped between my hipbones. Come to think of it, the clothes weren't so different from the ones today's parents (who wore them as kids!) condemn for prematurely "sexualizing" their daughters. The clothes were sexy then; they are sexy now. And to this day I can almost taste how good I felt in them. Before that summer, I still considered myself a little ugly and plenty awkward. In my high school, girls like me, who didn't have pageboy haircuts and didn't wear mohair sweaters with matching knee socks—and worse, who were smart—were untouchable.

At camp, though, I had suitors to spare. That summer several boys pursued me. One wore wire-rimmed glasses—avant-garde at the time. Another kept pleading with me to take my first acid trip with him. I was unmoved. I idolized the glamorous Jake, who had spent a year photographing guerrillas somewhere in Africa, who drove a battered Volkswagen, who meditated at an ashram. And he—miracle of miracles—liked me, a lot.

He liked *me*, I felt, and he saw *me*—saw the person I was beginning to know as myself. I could read his recognition in the photographs. They are straightforward, not arty, not pushy. I posed as I wanted; he shot. My body in them is at that heart-stopping stage between baby plump and adolescent fleshy. My face varies from picture to picture: Here I am a giggly kid, here a dreamy near-woman. One photo, which still hangs on my mother's wall, shows me holding Queen Anne's lace, gazing into the distance. It's a bit hokey: I'm working hard at looking soulful. But Jake's camera didn't mock. It's as if he believed I really was thinking deep thoughts.

What I was thinking about was sex. I tried to seduce him. In the flowery fields where we often went, I struck what I thought were enticing poses, leaning back in the long, scratchy grass, arching my back to reveal a bit of belly, dropping a shoulder so that a strap would fall invitingly off. In the little hand mirror I kept in my bunk, I rehearsed sucking in my cheeks and pouting my lips. And in the evergreen-smelling nights, I fantasized the day Jake would ask me to take my shirt off, brush his lips over my nipples, then pull down the short zipper of my pants. I imagined the bristles of his beard as he kissed me there.

Nothing Sexual Ever Happened

He never did. In fact, he mentioned sex only once that I remember, as I sat on the counter in his darkroom, watching his red-lit face concentrate on the images emerging in the trays (the smell of developing fluid is still erotic to me). He said, "There are two things I know I can't do while I'm working here: smoke pot or make love to a woman." Was that woman me? I closed my eyes for a second and imagined I was, pictured him stepping between my dangling legs, taking my face in his hands, and kissing me. I opened my eyes, unkissed.

Maybe Jake considered me a little girl, not a woman at all. But somehow, as he gazed at me through that lens, I began to see myself as a woman, at least a little. One hot sunny afternoon, shingling a roof with Jake and some other campers, I admired the muscles of his tan, bare back flexing with each hammer swing. The bitter-salty odor of his sweat drifted toward me on a breeze. "Hmm," I said to myself, smiling as I noticed that I liked the smell. "This must mean I'm growing up." Once, skinny-dipping, I felt my body go as liquid as the lake as I watched him climb onto the shore, the red-blond fuzz on his body beaded with water.

Today, camp policy, like that at many schools and community centers, might forbid Jake and me to spend those hours alone in a dark little room. The camp director might pull him aside and ask pointedly what we were doing out in the fields. A counselor might interrogate me about his actions and insinuate that he was exploiting me. She might even persuade me it was true.

Statutory rape laws are often unjust and unrealistic.

Of the dozens of rolls he photographed, there are a few shots of me with my shirt off, folk-dancing in a downpour with some other girls. I remember stepping back toward him, breathless and ecstatic, my face hot in the cool rain. "You're amazing," he said, and raised his camera again. Today those photographs could be called child pornography, and Jake could be arrested for taking them.

He never touched me, except to drape an arm over my shoulder or sit close to me on a bench. He kissed me on the lips only once, mouth closed, on the last day of camp—and gave his boots to another girl, throwing me into paroxysms of jealousy. But he made me feel beautiful. He made me feel desirable.

Society Has Become Suspicious of All Adults

Recently, the publication of my book *Harmful to Minors: The Perils of Protecting Children From Sex* lit a conflagration among conservatives, who called for its suppression—and called me an apologist for, even an advocate of, pedophilia. Why? In one chapter, I suggest that statutory rape laws are often unjust and unrealistic. They not only criminalize consensual teen relationships and categorically deny teens the right to consent to sex, they erase the very possibility that young people might desire—or initiate—sex at all, especially with an older person. At the same time, the book says, we've come to suspect all adults as sexual con artists, cajoling kids through popular culture and advertising to want sex, or seducing or coercing them to have it, before their time. It's as if adults, should they find a young person sexually appealing, could never control their impulses.

My book acknowledges that kids desire—and I know they do, because I did—and this apparently makes me a pedophile's patsy. Writing the book, I often felt lucky that I came of age during the brief moment when young people's sexuality was considered lovely and good and when adults who appreciated it were not regarded as perverts. In the summer of '67, a man gave a girl the innocent gift of her emerging erotic self. I wonder if I could receive it with such happiness and grace were I a girl today.

6

Teens Should Be Punished Legally for "Sexting"

Brent Bozell

Brent Bozell is the founder of the Media Research Center, a media watchdog organization, and he is a columnist for News Busters.org.

A new, dangerous trend among teenagers, called sexting, involves the sending of nude or semi-nude pictures via text message. In many states, prosecutors are punishing teens to the fullest extent of the law, with some being charged for possession of child pornography and having to register as sex offenders. Many experts and lawyers argue that these punishments are too harsh; however, others want the legal system to teach teens a lesson about the seriousness of their actions. Teens need to understand that these photos often do not remain between themselves and the intended recipient, and the effects of sexting can be far reaching, unhealthy, and sometimes tragic. One young girl committed suicide when her photo was passed around at four area high schools. The best way to teach teens that sexting is wrong is to prosecute them legally.

Can a child be accused of child pornography? Could a child then be formally charged and convicted of it? These are the questions raised by the disturbing new trend called "sexting," teenagers sending nude or semi-nude pictures around on their cell phones. In some jurisdictions, prosecutors are playing hardball, threatening that students caught

Brent Bozell, "The Sadness of Sexting," NewsBusters (NewsBusters.org), March 28, 2009. Reproduced by permission.

with naughty pictures could face jail time and being registered as sex offenders. At a minimum, prosecutors are demanding a 10-hour rehab program.

Does this offense seem too casual to justify throwing the legal book at children? Consider that it's undeniable that if Johnny was a day or two over 18 and was sending around these images, he'd be treated as a sicko—with prison time a real possibility.

Parents Are Fighting Back

In our litigious culture, it was only a matter of time: Now the "sexting" perpetrators are fighting back. In Wyoming County, Pennsylvania, three female students and their parents hired the American Civil Liberties Union [ACLU] to sue the county prosecutor for daring to suggest something wrong was done and insisting a ten-hour "re-education" program was necessary.

It's a thorny issue, to be sure. When legislators passed child-pornography laws, who could have imagined our culture would grow so decadent that children would be distributing nude pictures of themselves to other children? Who also would have predicted that some parents would be unashamed enough of their children's behavior to hire the ACLU and sue authorities for enforcing child-porn laws?

"Prosecutors should not be using a nuclear-weapon-type charge like child pornography against kids who have no criminal intent and are merely doing stupid things," proclaimed the ACLU lawyer, Witold Walczak.

But this is something that just cannot be dismissed as kids "doing stupid things."

"Sexting" Has Become Commonplace

"Sexting" has quickly grown from rare to commonplace. A survey of 1,280 teenagers and young adults released in December [2008] by the National Campaign to Prevent Teenage and Unplanned Pregnancy and CosmoGirl.com found that 20 percent of teenagers and 33 percent of young adults ages 20 to 26 said they had sent or posted nude or semi-nude photos of themselves.

The numbers were higher for the number who would admit they've received nude or semi-nude images: 31 percent of teens and 46 percent of young adults. They know it rarely stays private: 72 percent of teens and 68 percent of young adults agreed that sexy pictures often end up being "seen by more than the intended recipients."

When the subject of a "sexting" is famous, the image often ends up on the Internet. A nude photo of Vanessa Hudgens, the teenaged female star of Disney's "High School Musical" movies, went from private e-mail to Internet sensation.

"Sexting" Can Have Serious Repercussions

It can even end in suicide. *People* magazine reported that last year [in 2008], Jessie Logan, a senior at a Cincinnati-area high school, took a nude photo of herself and sent it to a boy she was dating. She then learned the photo was being distributed at four area high schools. Other students began taunting her as a "whore." She hanged herself.

Authorities aren't convicting children, but using the law as a teaching tool.

People's article on "sexting" cited the case of two 14-year-old boys in Massachusetts who received a photo of a 13-year-old girl exposing a breast. Parents were shocked that authorities were weighing child-pornography charges. Said one father: "What they did was wrong, but did they know it was wrong? . . . These are 14-year-old kids with 14-year-old minds, not adults."

Once parents get over the idea of seventh-grade girls flashing their private parts for the camera, it's clear that teenagers are not identical to adults who would prey on a 13-year-old. It's shocking to imagine ending up on the wrong side of the law by merely receiving an unsolicited pornographic image. Authorities aren't convicting children, but using the law as a teaching tool and trying to put a stop to a toxic new trend.

Some Experts Disagree

It's obvious that some experts will be quoted to defend it. The *Pittsburgh Post-Gazette* found Texas A&M professor Christopher Ferguson, who called the trend unwise, but "We would have done it, too, if we would have had the cool phones. We didn't do it because we didn't have the technology."

The same goes for defense attorneys. Public defender Dante Bertani protested a case of "sexting" teenagers in Greensburg, Pennsylvania: "Law enforcement gets carried away with what they believe is their duty to find everyone who spits on the sidewalk guilty of murder."

Bertani must not have heard of the Cincinnati suicide. He failed to acknowledge that spit on the sidewalk evaporates, but pornographic images can hang around forever on the "cool phones" and the Internet. Prosecutors and parents alike are correct to put the brakes on this mistake wherever it's discovered.

The civil libertarians may wish to reconsider their position. They claim it's a private matter best resolved by parental responsibility. Would it follow that their parental irresponsibility should make the parent the legally liable party?

7

"Sexting" Teens Should Be Punished by Parents, Not by the Legal System

Larry Magid

Larry Magid is a journalist and technology commentator. He is on the board of directors for the National Center for Missing and Exploited Children and has authored Child Safety for the Information Highway *and* Teen Safety on the Information Highway.

Sending a sexually explicit photo of yourself, especially when you are a teenager, is a dumb thing to do. Pictures can end up widely distributed, being seen by more than just the intended recipient. Teens sending or receiving explicit text messages also may face legal consequences. More and more teens are being charged with possession of child pornography and having to register as sex offenders because of sexting. Laws that were created to protect children are the same laws that are now being used to punish teens for using poor judgment. Sexting is a teenage fad that will eventually lose its popularity; but until then, instead of passing new laws or misusing the ones we already have, we should let teens' parents handle sexting situations.

Sexting is the practice of taking a sexually revealing picture of yourself, typically from a cell phone, and sending it to someone. Legal consequences aside, it's a dumb thing to do, especially as a teen fad.

Larry Magid, "Sexting Can Be Big Legal Trouble For Teens," *SiliconValley* (siliconvalley.com), April 7, 2009. Reproduced by permission.

Even if you are comfortable with the person receiving the image, you never know for sure where else it might go. Digital images are easy to copy and forward and—even if you trust your friend's discretion—it can be accidentally forwarded or seen by others with access to your friend's phone or computer. It's not uncommon for such images to find their way to other people's cell phones and even Web pages, where they can be seen by anyone, copied, searched for and redistributed, perhaps forever.

There Are Legal Consequences

For minors, there's another risk—serious legal consequences. Creating, transmitting and even possessing a nude, semi-nude or sexually explicit image of a minor can be considered child pornography. It can be prosecuted as a state or federal felony and can even lead to having to register as a sex offender.

Crazy as it seems, some prosecutors have gone after teens for taking and sending pictures of themselves.

There was a case in Florida a couple of years ago [in 2007] where a teenage boy and girl photographed themselves nude and engaged in "unspecified sexual behavior." One kid sent the picture to the other and somehow the police got involved. They were tried and convicted for production and distribution of child porn; the teen who received the image had the additional charge of possession. An appeals court upheld the convictions.

Three teenage girls from Pennsylvania were charged [in] January [2009] for creating child porn and the three boys who received the images were charged for possessing it. The judge in that case tried to temporarily block the prosecutor from filing child pornography charges while he considered the merits of the case.

A Texas eighth-grader spent a night in jail in October [2008] after a coach found a nude picture on his cell phone, sent by another student, according to a CBS News report.

It's sadly ironic that the very child porn laws written to protect children from being exploited by adults could wind up having a devastating impact on the lives of children who, while acting stupidly, have no criminal intent.

The Main Cause Is Peer Pressure

It's hard to know how prevalent the practice is. But if you believe the results of an online survey commissioned by the National Campaign to Prevent Teen and Unplanned Pregnancy, about 22 percent of teenage girls and 18 percent of boys admit to having "electronically sent, or posted online, nude or semi-nude pictures or video of themselves."

Kids aren't stupid and, faced with the facts, most will wise up.

I'm not completely confident about the [study] results, which was carried out by a market research firm and not subject to academic peer review, but I think it's fair to assume that a significant number of children are doing this.

Perhaps more interesting than the survey's overall number is the breakdown of why teens take and send these pictures. Of those who reportedly sent such pictures, 71 percent of girls and 67 percent of boys said they sent content to a boyfriend or girlfriend, while 21 percent of the girls and 39 percent of the boys say they sent it to someone they wanted to date.

As you might expect, peer pressure plays a role. Of those who sent such content, 51 percent of teen girls cited "pressure from a guy," while 18 percent of teen boys blamed pressure from girls.

"Sexting" Will Go Away

While sexting is troubling, I think it's important for us all to take a deep breath and refrain from passing new laws or using child pornography laws that were designed to protect children from exploitation by adults.

I suspect that sexting will diminish over time. Kids aren't stupid and, faced with the facts, most will wise up. We also know that kids who get in trouble online are the same kids who get in trouble offline, so when teens repeatedly do sexting or other stupid or risky things online, it's important to intervene early and often.

The best thing for a parent to do is to have a non-confrontational conversation—perhaps over dinner—to ask your kids if they've heard about sexting and what they think about it. You might not get a straight answer but you'll open up a dialog that can go a long way toward helping your kids understand how to minimize legal, social and reputation risks.

8

Sexually Active Teens Are Unfairly Labeled as Criminals

Niki Delson

Niki Delson, a licensed clinical social worker for more than twenty-five years, specializes in helping victims of sexual abuse. She recently has begun a treatment program for the rehabilitation of sex offenders.

Americans are obsessed with and fearful about sex, and young people are receiving mixed messages as a result. For example, at age twelve, youths can consent to an abortion and receive birth control pills, but they are not legally permitted to have sex until they are sixteen, or even eighteen, depending on the state where they live. Many of the laws written to protect children often do more harm than good, punishing teens for sexual behavior that is actually normal. American culture sensationalizes sex for profit, so much so that society becomes desensitized to it, which pushes the media to find even more sexually disturbing stories to keep America watching. This vicious cycle in turn creates moral panic among groups that become overly sensitized to sexually explicit material, and thereby make it their mission to seek to punish those who threaten their beliefs and way of life. Society does not want to believe that male interest in teenage girls is normal behavior or that a teen's sexual relationship with an adult is not always harmful.

Sex! We are obsessed, stimulating ourselves through the media, exposing ourselves to nonstop sexual images, using sex to sell everything from shaving cream to children's underwear. We are also horrified by our concerns with sexual abuse, child molesters, sexually transmitted diseases and a belief that sexual expression in childhood may lead to sexual misbehavior in adolescence and adult sexual offending. Our obsession with and horror about sex, have paradoxically generated both great sexual freedom and draconian laws, which unfortunately have several (largely unintended) negative consequences. These may be summarized as follows:

1. Legal age of consent is out of sync with normal sexual development, and adolescents are given conflicting and many confusing messages about sexual behavior. For example, they can generally consent to abortion and obtain birth control at age 12 but cannot consent to sex until 16 or 18 (depending on the state). As a result, many are being convicted of felonies for developmentally normal behaviors and having to register as sex offenders for the remainder of their lives.

2. Pre-pubescent children are being ostracized (and occasionally even criminalized) for sexual behavior that is often normal or at worst, an annoying means of attention seeking.

3. Mandatory child abuse reporting laws, originally designed to protect children have been expanded to identifying offenders, making it virtually impossible for them to enter treatment on their own initiative without first suffering severe legal consequences.

4. Under the guise of "protecting our communities," without a shred of empirical support and in spite of significant empirical evidence to the contrary, sex offenders who served their sentences are being forced to leave their homes (and sometimes families) because they live

too close to schools, playgrounds or parks. In most instances destabilizing these men is patently unfair and in some cases it tends to make them more rather than less dangerous. . . .

Laws Are Out of Sync with Puberty

Beginning with puberty (average age around 12), sexual thoughts and urges become increasingly stronger and more frequent. Exploring, expressing and learning to manage sexuality is one of the most important developmental tasks of the teenage years and occasional behavior based on poor judgment is obviously inevitable. But the age of consent, which varies somewhat from state to state, is out of sync with normal sexual development in every state. Consequently, adolescents are increasingly being charged with felonies for ordinary, consensual and developmentally normal behaviors. Consider the situation reported by Pamela Manson of the *Salt Lake City Tribune*.

Normal adolescent sexual behaviors have been classified as illegal activities.

Utah Supreme Court justices acknowledged Tuesday [May 29, 2007] that they were struggling to wrap their minds around the concept that a 13-year-old Ogden girl could be both an offender and a victim for the same act—in this case, having consensual sex with her 12-year-old boyfriend.

The girl was put in this odd position because she was found guilty of violating a state law that prohibits sex with someone under age 14. She also was the victim in the case against her boyfriend, who was found guilty of the same violation by engaging in sexual activity with her.

Clearly, normal adolescent sexual behaviors have been classified as illegal activities, often labeled "deviant" and therefore worthy of punishment and treatment.

Teens Are Having Sex Anyway

Before we start labeling sexually active teens as deviant, it would be helpful to know what is considered "normal" sexual behavior for adolescents. The dictionary definition of "deviant" is:

> deviating or departing from the norm; characterized by deviation: deviant social behavior. Or a person whose behavior deviates from what is acceptable especially in sexual behavior [syn: pervert]

According to the Child Trends Data Bank:

1. Among young people ages 15 to 24 in 2002, 13 percent of females and 5 percent of males reported that their first sexual experience occurred at age 15 or younger with an individual who was three or more years older.

2. In 2002, approximately 2.5% of teens ages 15 to 19 who had not had sexual intercourse, engaged in oral sex with an opposite sex partner.

3. In 2005, 47% of high school students had experienced sexual intercourse. The percentage of students who are sexually experienced increases by grade. In 2005, 34 percent of ninth graders had ever had sexual intercourse, compared with 63 percent of twelfth graders.

Age of Consent Laws were originally written to protect children from forced prostitution. Even 1890's reformers recognized that prosecuting post-pubescent teenagers was not only senseless but undermined the intention of protective legislation.

The Society (for the Prevention of Cruelty to Children) concerned itself only with those under the age of sixteen years, arguing that by that age the onset of puberty would have occurred, bringing with it the physical strength and "higher intelligence and greater strength of will" that distinguished adults from children.

When campaigns by other purity reformers succeeded in raising the age of consent to eighteen years, Elbridge Gerry, the NYSPCC [New York Society for the Prevention of Cruelty to Children] President, complained that the age was now set beyond the time when "a girl became a woman." Not only would it be impossible to obtain any convictions in cases that involved the sixteen and seventeen year old girls, he lamented, but the effort to prosecute such cases would undermine the legitimacy of the law, making it more difficult to win convictions in cases involving girls under the age of sixteen (late 19th Century).

Consent Laws Are Misused

But now these same laws are being used to criminalize virtually all teenage sexuality. One can certainly argue that engaging in sex is not good for teens because it risks unwanted pregnancy, STD's [sexually transmitted diseases], and social/emotional entanglements they may have difficulty managing. However for all the reasons Elbridge Gerry foresaw and some he didn't, criminalizing the behavior is one of the worst possible strategies for protecting them. Do we REALLY want to prosecute the 14 year old Utah girl and make her into a lifelong registered sex offender? Is she THAT dangerous?

Criminalizing normative teenage sexual behavior has the unfortunate outcome of placing sexually active teens on the same sex offender registry as predatory pedophiles. For example, 18 year old Joshua Lunsford, the brother of Jessica Lunsford, for whom Jessica's Laws are named, was recently arrested for "unlawful sexual conduct" with a 14 year old. If convicted, he will be required to register under the same laws as John Couey—his sister's murderer.

Or, ponder the fate of Genarlow Wilson, who at age 17 had consensual oral sex with his 15 year old girlfriend. For this "felony" he is presently serving 10 years without possibility of parole in a Georgia prison.

What makes this case more absurd is that if Mr. Wilson and the young woman had sexual intercourse, he would have been guilty only of a misdemeanor and not required to register as a sex offender, thanks to a provision in the law meant to avoid just this type of draconian punishment for consensual youthful indiscretions, the "Romeo and Juliet" exception.

Our culture sensationalizes sex for profit.

As Wilson's trial was unfolding, a 27-year-old teacher was being found guilty just down the hall of sex with a 17-year-old student—the kind of crime for which child molestation statutes were written. She got three years of probation and 90 days in jail.

Moral Groups Make the Situation Worse

Our culture sensationalizes sex for profit ... whether we are selling clothing, toys television shows or 24/7 infotainment. One problem with this is that it's a kind of "addiction". Over time we become increasingly numbed to content that once excited us, so we demand more and better. Maintaining viewer interest requires the media to constantly find new things to alarm us. The end result has been moral panic about all sexual misbehavior. (If we were meth addicts instead of sexual infotainment addicts, we'd be "tweaking" at this point.)

Moral panics have been described as a condition, episode, person or group of persons, which emerge to become defined as a threat to societal values and interests. These threats are designed in a sensationalized fashion by the media as well as other agents of social control, including politicians, law enforcement and religious leaders, with the intention of establishing meaningful parameters for acceptable societal behavior.

Moral panics then, are those processes whereby members of a society and culture become 'morally sensitized' to the challenges and menaces posed to 'their' accepted values and ways of life, by the activities of groups defined as deviant. The process underscores the importance of the mass media in providing, maintaining and 'policing' the available frameworks and definitions of deviance, which structure both public awareness of, and attitudes toward, social problems.

Society Has Allowed This to Happen

So who are WE in the matter? We have become complacent and satisfied with expressing our outrage without exploring how we contribute to it. Advertisers use sex to sell products because WE buy more when they do. We watch "To Catch a Predator" and feel comforted to know that [NBC News *Dateline* correspondent] Chris Hansen and Perverted Justice have already exposed 200 potential child abusers. But the producers don't ask us to consider what it says about human nature that so many men, even with the notoriety of the show, will seek out a sexual encounter with a teen. The audience would probably shrink away with the first mention that male sexual interest in teenage girls is normal or that research does not support that teens are always harmed by sexual experiences with an adult.

Movie legend Kirk Douglas became a willing victim of statutory rape when he lost his virginity to a school teacher aged just 15. In his forthcoming autobiography *Let's Face It—90 Years of Living, Loving and Learning*, the veteran actor confesses he didn't realise his lover could face prison for their affair, but still doesn't regret a thing. Recalling the tryst he writes, "I had been a ragamuffin kid of 15 coping with a neighbourhood filled with gangs. . . . Under her guidance I became a different person. I am eternally grateful. By today's standards she would have gone to jail. I had no idea we were doing something wrong. Did she?"

But that conversation is not popular and not widely engaged in, at least openly. The blueprint for "To Catch a Predator", for the politics around sexual crimes, for the exceedingly harsh penalties for sexual misbehavior is in the message that we need to watch out for "them" not "us." As long as we [shape the] language [of] the dialogue in this fashion we will continue down the path of creating more victims than we protect. Just ask Genarlow Wilson, Josh Lundsford, and a 14-year old girl in Utah who we are "protecting" by withholding her name while ruining her life.

9

Morally Driven Groups Should Be Tempered in Age of Consent Issues

Maria-Belen Ordonez

Maria-Belen Ordonez is a professor of social anthropology at York University in Ontario, Canada, and a member of Toronto's Sex Laws Committee.

John Robin Sharpe is being punished for having a consensual sexual relationship with a boy more than twenty years ago, and it is because there is no statute of limitations on crimes of desire in Canada. The boy posed in pictures for Sharpe when he was eleven years old, and that later led to a sexual relationship. The boy, now thirty-five, has joined the bandwagon of moral crusaders who are now trying to prosecute Sharpe, even though he admits that he "liked" Sharpe, giving the impression that he has fond memories of the relationship. However, the man's views changed now that he is an adult and has children of his own, and he now feels that he must abide by society's rules of what is acceptable and unacceptable sexual behavior. Adding to the pressure to conform to these rules are the many moral groups that are taking their stand against Sharpe. Society needs to question who these moral groups are and what right they have to decide who society fears and who they should trust.

John Robin Sharpe—a notorious name in the imagination of Canadians and a name that has had a disturbing and constant presence in the minds of the morally righteous. Even

Maria-Belen Ordonez, "How Robin Sharpe Became the Devil," Xtra.ca, August 5, 2004. Reproduced by permission.

those who admit supporting a good legal challenge, feel they must, out of a vague conviction, abide by decisions that "draw the line" when dealing with issues of consent and sex laws in general.

Drawing the line is what I have often heard when I've spoken of Sharpe's legal challenges around Canada's child pornography laws and most current sexual assault conviction for events that happened more than 30 years ago.

Defending freedom of speech can validate the right of Sharpe to produce photographs of young men and boys and his SM [sadomasochism, a form of sexual role playing] writing because the courts have said that they have artistic merit. But Sharpe's legal battle over an alleged sexual assault on a boy has many Canadians drawing the line, and others outright celebrating their heroic efforts to obliterate "child" pornography and to undo everything that Sharpe, 71, represents.

Their Relationship Was Consensual

Crusades to save children unfold in many ways and sometimes the mere connection of children and sex inspires a renewed trust in the courts, a renewed trust in consent laws and a now popular reliance on the idea that boys don't know what they're doing in the hands of old "dirty men" (who are de facto in positions of authority and trust).

Legal scrutiny is not something that the majority have or want access to.

Sharpe's recent legal battle involves one of these boys who not only posed for Sharpe's camera but who developed a consensual relationship with him more than 20 years ago. Since there is no statute of limitations on crimes of desire, the now 35-year-old man joined the band of crusaders to undo a part of his life, a public admittance that returns him to an age of innocence whereby he can point to the nation's favourite paedophile and complete the legal crucifixion.

Yet Sharpe's two-year prison sentence on this charge will hopefully inspire us to ask questions about the harshness of the sentence, given the nature of their relationship and the testimony of the 35-year-old man in March of [2004], who admits to having "liked" Sharpe, "but if somebody did that to [his] kids, [he'd] want to kill him."

"Liking" Sharpe is directly connected to being an 11-year-old boy and having memories of the relationship that aren't negative. The moral position to defend his children comes from a 35-year-old father who admits his earlier transgression of social rules and behaviours, only to later in life abide by social norms.

A Crusading Detective

What does this moral position, this social norm currently look like? Who partakes in assuring that moral positions about non-abusive, non-coercive relationships merit criminal convictions? Legal scrutiny is not something that the majority have or want access to. Instead we are left with media sound bites. The outcome is further moral panic about young persons and sex, and a disconnection from a social world that actually fuels ideas of abuse about intergenerational relationships under the guise of "protecting" children.

After Sharpe was acquitted by the Supreme Court in 2002 for his SM literary work, it didn't take long before the morally concerned jumped in to try and save the nation, exemplified by the introduction of Bill C-12, which basically attempted to eradicate the artistic merit defence, which helped Sharpe win that case.

Det[ective] Noreen Waters is representative of this mission. She has been commended by the Vancouver Police Force and honoured in 2002 for her persistence to introduce new charges, the assault charges, that would convict Sharpe once and for all. She's also been commended by rightwing groups like Focus On The Family, who praise her efforts as extraordinary because of who she is: a mother, a wife and a detective who despises everything that Sharpe represents—an older gay man who likes boys. It is ultimately Waters who searched out the now 35-year-old man. On one website she takes solace in her family: "I have a nice home, I do crafts, I make brooches out of antique pieces of jewellery and I teach Sunday school."

If there isn't abuse then maybe evoking something in between will carry the same weight.

Is it possible to expect Waters and those who support her to consider an alternative that might actually make a distinction between real abuse, coercion, harm, consensual relationships, photographs and literary writing?

The Moral Group's Powerful Influence

The point here is to question the sound bites that appear as headlines. Take Rosalind Prober, the president of a group called Beyond Borders, who has been in the courts as a "friend" of the prosecution. This particular nonprofit organization against child pornography clearly states on its website that intervening in court cases is a priority because, apparently, "children come first." Furthermore, their moral position already privileges their presence and input in the courts most certainly beyond any possible contribution that may come from alternative voices.

It is no wonder that the media flashes pay particular attention to the opinions of Prober, who, after Sharpe's July 19 [2004] sentencing, vaguely referred to Sharpe as an "example of the link between child pornography and child abuse." What does this actually mean? What is this space between child pornography and child abuse? The vagueness stems from a strange recognition that if there isn't abuse then maybe evoking something in between will carry the same weight. Maybe naming Sharpe as that link will socially situate a new breed of sexual outcasts, those who continue to defy and continue to fight (via appeals) without shame, and as the Crown's lawyer put it "without remorse."

Society Should Be More Critical of These Groups

Whether we understand or want to understand Sharpe, we need to question the extent to which the most recent conviction is morally inspired and to place our critique on organizations such as Beyond Borders who have the authority and the voice to tell us what moral links we should fear.

The question here is not whether Sharpe's relationship with the plaintiff was socially acceptable or repulsive, or whether the partial truths of the media should have a determining impact on how we respond. We need to respond with a cynicism that situates morally driven organizations in this country as the main instigators of panic and fear and expose their apparent good deeds as the real threat to democratic citizenship.

10

Age of Consent Laws Must Be Reviewed and Revised

Laurie Peterson

Laurie Peterson is the spokesperson for Moral Outrage, a group that is fighting for the reform of statutory rape laws.

The same government that sends teens to school together and teaches them about safe sex also makes it illegal for them to engage in sex. This is confusing teens, giving them the message that if they are being taught to be safe about sex, then it must be legal. However, many of these children are finding out the hard way that this is not the case, and some are being convicted for having sex with someone in their own peer group and are being forced to become registered sex offenders. Because of the social stigma attached to the label of "sex offender," many politicians are unwilling to look at reforming these laws that were put into place decades ago when teen sex was not as prevalent. Thus, innocent teenagers who have no criminal intentions continue to be punished.

Consensual teenaged sexual experimentation is an activity that is labeled by most states as child sexual abuse, child molestation, sexual assault and statutory rape. Under most state laws it is a felony crime, accompanied by sex offender registration. The legislative belief is that these relationships are coercive and unhealthy even if they are consensual.

Most local governments send teenagers to high school from freshman to senior year, ranging in age from 14 to 19 on

Laurie Peterson, "A Lifetime of Shame for Consensual Sex," MoralOutrage.net, July 27, 2007. Reproduced by permission.

average. Ironically, these same state governments make it explicitly illegal for these peers to engage in some, if not all, forms of consensual sexual relations. These adolescents are taught a safe sex message in school, even as under-aged minors, who cannot legally engage in sexual intercourse. These minors in turn have a tendency to equate safe sex with legal sex and they are wrong, sometimes with lifelong consequences. While it is the general intent of statutory rape laws across the nation to discourage underage sexual activity, is it the equal intent of these laws to subject these young offenders to a lifetime of stigma by registration? In light of the seriousness of a felony record and registration requirements it is time to review the parameters of these laws and the consequences they have for youth at the dawn of their adult lives.

Adolescents are taught a safe sex message in school, even as under-aged minors, who cannot legally engage in sexual intercourse.

Decades ago when these laws were first pieced together the outcome was much different for a statutory rape conviction than it is today. The outcome during that time was a criminal record unencumbered by the release of [Criminal Offender Record Information, or] CORI reports and registration requirements. After their conception, sexual assault laws were coupled with new legislation that further compounded a conviction. Federal legislation expanded the release of criminal records reports under the Fair Credit Reporting Act (15 USC 1681g, et seq.) used by employers and subsequently resulted in the direct loss of employment for young offenders. In addition, Federal laws like the Wetterling Act, Megan's Law and The Adam Walsh Act have now mandated lengthy registration periods and online posting of information under the title of "Sex Offender or Offender Against Children" and these newer laws have resulted in a social stigma and a private shame for young offenders that could not possibly have been anticipated by legislators when the original sexual assault laws were created. Today sex crime convictions equate directly with job loss and [reduced] employment opportunities, possible residency restrictions, and a general inability to provide for a future family through gainful employment and parental involvement (volunteering, coaching, and chaperoning) in the lives of future children. Registration laws at their heart were aimed at violent and predatory sex offenders, not teenage love affairs or casual nights of experimentation. It is time to restore balance to the system by removing these young men and women from the registry for their consensual sex acts as teenagers.

The Truth in Statistics

A significant number of teenagers are engaging in all types of sex acts well below the age of consent. Sexual assault laws generally define penetration as any object, however slight, that penetrates the sex organ of another. Many teens are involved in acts of mutual groping that could fall under the legal definition of penetration, without actually having sexual intercourse, and thus would be guilty of statutory rape. One shudders to think what the outcome would be if there was a nationwide attempt to crack down on this 'heinous' criminal activity inside the walls of our high schools. It's hard to imagine the courts would have time to prosecute anything else. While this group of registered sex offenders represents the minority of those registered, there are still substantial numbers of young men and women forced to register for consensual sex as adolescents and society should not overlook them.

Complicating statutory rape law review is the associated label of 'sex offender'. Families are bombarded with messages daily assailing sex offenders as a group. They are touted as the 'worst of the worst', untreatable monsters who will repeat their crimes. With such an ugly stain attached to the sex offender label, there is little doubt as to why politicians back off from endorsing any sort of meaningful and necessary reform to sex offender laws. Perception being nine tenths of the law, all registered sex offenders must be child molesters. The truth it seems is rarely reported. The truth is that those guilty of statutory rape would not have been guilty of a crime at all in a specified number of days (when the underage partner turned the legal age). It underscores the reality that maturity cannot be legislated in black and white terms. Those convicted of statutory rape are rarely repeat offenders, though there are little studies to prove this because these young adults rarely serve prison time, and most studies are conducted on those who have been paroled since prison sentences indicate a more serious offense. Even those guilty of other types of sex crimes are not as likely to repeat these offenses as society has been led to believe. The US Dept of Justice issued a study in 2003 that followed just under 10,000 convicted sex offenders released from prison in 1994. Less than 400, approx 3.5% were returned to prison for a repeat sex offense within the first three years following release. This hardly represents the 'high rate of recidivism' that is loudly proclaimed by those looking to advance their political standing with tough new laws aimed at registered sex offenders.

An Uncomfortable Topic of Debate

Interestingly, women's and children's rights advocates have asserted that a level of coercion exists based on the age difference alone between two consenting teens and thus a sexual assault has occurred regardless of the consent given. These powerful lobbying groups, along with victim's rights advocates, are unwilling to acknowledge that an 18, 19 or 20 year old can be both an adolescent and an adult simultaneously and lack criminal intent when it comes to sexual relations with a younger partner. Their belief is that these individuals are undeniably adults and therefore should know better than to engage with an underage peer under all circumstances.

While the potential age difference represents an aspect of the debate that makes many uncomfortable, some criminal penalties for statutory rape do not have to be removed in order to accomplish reform. Allowing judicial discretion in sentencing for this age group, as well as removing the registration requirements for a first time offense, would suffice. These organizations continue to strongly oppose these changes alleging that these 'mature adults' use their older age status to manipulate younger individuals into relationships with them. These groups refuse to acknowledge that the younger partner may have wanted, provoked or encouraged this attention and they disregard younger partners who insist they are not victims. In fact the very idea is dismissed as blaming the victim or oneself if the older person in the sexual relationship is not held completely and solely accountable for the sex acts that occurred. These advocacy groups continue to hinder the potential reform of statutory rape laws by not allowing any open dialogue that can weigh and balance the aspects of accountability and maturity on both sides of this contentious subject.

Innocent Teens Are Being Wrongly Labeled

The current imbalance of accountability is most evident in the strict liability nature of statutory rape laws. Statutory rape laws are defined as strict liability crimes in 33 states. Strict liability means that the prosecution does not have to prove criminal intent, only that the criminal act occurred. Victim advocacy groups stress the need for the 'strict' protection offered by these laws in an attempt to save young teenage individuals from their own poor decisions. There is no such protection afforded to older teenage individuals in these situations. Consequently, the impact of this type of law is that there have been mentally innocent people convicted of statutory rape with a peer they believed to be 'of age'. It is not a defense in court to say that the underage minor misrepresented their age in most states. The result of this strict liability is that innocent minds that did not intend to commit a crime are irrelevant before a court of law. There is little push to change this imbalance because it is poorly understood by the public and once an individual is labeled a sex offender, they are no longer part of mainstream society, regardless of the nature of their crime. Young adults and older teens have painfully little life experience and may not realize that they are being lied to by someone they perceive as a peer. Even worse, they have no concept of strict liability crimes and their automatic guilt under the law because they have barely entered adulthood and are lacking the critical knowledge that these circumstances exist.

This transition into adulthood should not be overlooked when reviewing statutory rape laws. For most teens this is a complicated and tumultuous time, of still being 'a child' while simultaneously being allowed several 'adult' privileges. In [New Hampshire], as in most states, the first adult privilege our children receive is a driver's license at age 16. Their adult privileges continue to grow until the age of 21 when they are legally able to buy and consume alcohol. In legal terms, I would argue [New Hampshire] has defined the age range of 16 to 21 as the age of transition for our youth into adulthood. Even insurance companies regard the age of maturity as 25 years old when deciding on premium decreases. This age range makes notoriously poor decisions, as most of us know from our own personal experiences. There is scientific research to support the assertion that the age range for adolescence is markedly longer than previously regarded, lasting well into the early twenties. Do people really need to be reminded that teens and young adults have bad judgment without necessarily having criminal intent? A great number of our own actions during those transition years could be considered regrettable to say the least. It is easy to imagine how our own lives may have been different if we were subject to prosecution for consensual experimentation.

Consent Laws Must Be Reviewed

As the wife of an offender who is registered for life over a night of consensual sex as a teen, I can tell you this is an outrage. My husband and children have been shunned by others in the neighborhood because the perception is that all sex offenders are child molesters. My husband is not alone. Genarlow Wilson of Atlanta, Georgia, is currently serving a ten year prison sentence for receiving consensual oral sex at the age of 17, from a 15 year old peer, and will be registered for life upon his release. A quick search on the internet will confirm that millions of people around America have rallied around Genarlow to voice their disgust in his sentence and to call for his release. The media and public outrage in Genarlow's situation is rare, and most do not get the same support. Joshua Widner is another young man who is sitting in prison for ten years, convicted of the same crime as Genarlow and it has sparked no outrage. Perhaps it is because there was a slightly larger age gap in Joshua Widner's case than there was in Genarlow Wilson's case. The net result is still the same: a young man in prison for a mandatory ten years over a consensual sex act. Some of these teens, labeled by the law as a victim, are now married to their partners who are registering as sex offenders and considered their abusers by our criminal justice system. Take, for example, [New Hampshire's] own Jody Barry and his wife. Jody is registered as a sex offender and posted online for life. Kearstin is the victim, and the mother of their four children. It's been more than ten years since they were teenagers, but their lives are still shadowed by the law. She was fourteen, pretending to be older; he was eighteen and believed she told him the truth. There is no relief in the law for this couple and there is no relief for anyone else convicted under consensual circumstances either.

Until statutory rape laws and associated registration laws are examined there will be no relief. In reviewing these laws and registration requirements, it is necessary to remember that registration laws are not about punishment; they are about public safety. The US Supreme Court ruled in *SMITH V. DOE* (2003) that sex offender registration was not a punitive sanction, establishing that these laws were not intended to be used as punishment. Registration laws pass constitutional muster because they were determined by the Supreme Court to be civil regulations imposed by the government for a narrowly defined interest in protecting the public safety. The original intent of registration laws was narrowly defined in the beginning but it has grown to encompass perfectly natural sex acts amongst adolescents. It is perfectly acceptable, psychologically speaking, to be aroused by your own social group during your teen years. Those who fall in this category do not pose an immediate threat. The offenders who ought to cause concern are those who are abnormally aroused by abnormal things. Labeling these young men and women as sex offenders for consensual sex acts inflicts immeasurable trauma on these young individuals as they contemplate their new reality as child molesters in society. Thoughts of suicide are common for those convicted under these circumstances. Even though they did not molest children, the title sex offender is synonymous and the psychological damage of this label is huge. There exists a widely recognized problem of childhood sexual abuse. However, those unfairly labeled as child molesters continue to go unrecognized and grouped in with a broad range of registered sex offenders that no one would dare defend.

A significant number of teenagers are engaging in all types of sex acts well below the age of consent.

Other Effects of Consent Laws

In trying to remedy the problem created by registering teens and young adults as sex offenders for consensual sexual activity, state's have three options: allow petitions for removal, craft the laws to make this activity legal, or continue to make these acts illegal and do not couple convictions with registration laws for a first offense. It is time to realize that having the wrong people on the sex offender registry risks hurting the whole community in many ways. It cannot be stressed enough that the inclusion of those who have lesser, non-violent and singular offenses on the registry is a benefit to those with violent and predatory offenses. These dangerous offenders are harder to spot and track when everyone is included under the same umbrella of lifetime registration and online posting. Further, it unfairly lowers the property values for citizens living near a registered offender, so it would make sense to keep the list of registered offenders narrow and specific. Lastly, our tax dollars are best spent registering and monitoring high risk offenders who have repeated their crimes, or have shown excessive violence, or have multiple prepubescent victims, rather than squandering resources on consensual sex acts engaged in by pubescent adolescents that lack the criminal intent of an older adult grooming a young teen for sexual purposes. Comprehensive review and subsequent reform is long overdue.

11

Underage Sex Is as Bad for Boys as for Girls

Deborah Orr

Deborah Orr is a British journalist and broadcaster. She also has worked as an editor for the Guardian Weekend *magazine and is currently a columnist for* The Independent.

Many people, including lawmakers and judges, do not consider boys who have underage sex as victims, even when the sexual act is with someone twice their age. Because society views boys, some of whom are as young as fourteen, as sexual predators, some people fail to see the negative impacts that sexual relationships have on them. However, girls and women alike are consistently treated as victims, instead of as the sexual predators they can be. The law should treat all children equally, whether boys or girls, and punish any adult who has sex with a child under the age of consent.

It's ridiculous to suggest a 14-year-old boy is a predator, while a girl is a victim.

It is not helpful to describe [Sharon] Edwards as "walking free" from court. The 40-year-old pleaded guilty this week [October 2008] to four charges of sexual activity with a child, and one of offering to supply Class A drugs. She may not indeed be in jail, but nor is she entirely at liberty.

Edwards received a 12-month suspended sentence and was ordered to register as a sex offender for five years. Further, Edwards has been thoroughly named, and thoroughly shamed. Due largely to the extraordinary summing up given by the judge in the case, Peter Fox QC, her crimes have been widely reported. The judge accepted that Edwards had been, "a very unhappy lady for a very considerable period of time when this 14-year-old boy seduced you, and not you him, both so far as sexual matters and drugs are concerned".

It is widely considered . . . that boys simply cannot be "taken advantage of."

Children's charities have been quick to condemn the remarks of the judge, as well they might. It is not unusual for boys or girls to develop fixations on adults, and it is preposterous to suggest that it is the fault of the child if the object of their desires happens to be an adult who is unable, for whatever reason, to deal appropriately with such a situation. Intercourse with a minor is illegal, and Edwards' guilty plea suggests that she understands this better than the judge does. It is the attitude of the judge, rather than the sentence Edwards has received, that is the troubling aspect of this case.

Even though Edwards is not a teacher, but a housewife, her case does have echoes of the Amy Gehring case six years ago [2002], in which the supply teacher was acquitted after having sexual encounters with several pupils, including intercourse with a 16-year-old. Gehring had become "friends" with a cohort of her pupils, and insisted that: "These boys weren't stupid. They knew what they were doing. I know the law's there to protect children from criminal activity. They knew what they were doing."

Gehring's case attracted wide publicity, with many people in agreement with the biology teacher that most boys who discovered that an older woman was willing to have sex with them, would simply count themselves lucky, and that no harm could possibly have been done to them. It is widely considered—and this seems to be a view shared by Judge Peter Fox—that boys simply cannot be "taken advantage of".

Yet boys most certainly can be, as the harrowing details of a recent television documentary, *Chosen*, attest. In this film three men who had attended the highly regarded Caldicott prep school, in Buckinghamshire, told of the systematic grooming and abuse they had endured at the school during the 1960s and 1970s.

All of them had felt as though they were part of a special elite of favoured children while the abuse was occurring, and did not fully realise how greatly they had been damaged until they were older. One of them, who had waited until his parents had died before he pursued justice, eventually succeeded in securing a conviction against his abuser, who all those years later had still been teaching.

Each of these men explains that the abuse visited on him as a child has had a profound and damaging effect on the rest of his life, and there is little reason to dispute this. But of course, few people do tend to dispute whether sexual abuse can damage young teenagers when the abuse is homosexual.

I doubt whether Judge Peter Fox would have dared, in the current climate, even to have suggested that a 40-year-old man was the innocent party, had he been knowingly "seduced" by either a 14-year-old girl or a 14-year-old boy. The attitudes of the judge suggest a fearful contempt for males, who are old enough at 14 to be routinely considered as sophisticated sexual predators.

Yet they also suggest a patronising contempt for females, whose mere "unhappiness" is enough to excuse the vulnerable creatures when they are unable to behave like adults. And they insult children most, of course, because they flout the idea that until they are 16, they deserve to be protected by the law.

The really worrying thing is that the judge's awful perspective reflects a widespread confusion, in law and in wider society, about children, adults and sexual matters. At the time of her encounters Gehring was not breaking the law by having sex with a 16-year-old pupil, even though she was a teacher. Before she came to trial though, in 2002, it was made an offence "for any person in a position of trust and responsibility to have any form of sexual relations with someone under 18 who is in their care".

Yet not everyone is happy with this situation either. Earlier in the month, Chris Keates, general secretary of the NASUWT [largest teacher's union in the United Kingdom], questioned whether it was right that teachers entering into relationships with people over the age of sexual consent should be branded, technically, as sex offenders. He argues that: "This isn't a person who is showing any tendencies for being a sex offender; this is a person who has made a serious error of professional judgement."

It's ridiculous to suggest that a 14-year-old schoolboy is a sexual predator, but that an 18-year-old schoolgirl cannot possibly know her own mind.

Oddly, it is this particular case, which involved neither a teacher, nor a young adult aged between 16 and 18, that illustrates most forcefully all that is wrong with this idea that the policing of relationships between people who are fully adult and people who can still be regarded as vulnerable can be chopped and changed according to the job that an adult does.

First, it is crucial that the law treats all children equally. It's ridiculous to suggest that a 14-year-old schoolboy is a sexual predator, but that an 18-year-old schoolgirl cannot possibly know her own mind. The age of sexual consent is 16, and any adult who abuses that legal boundary must be held responsible for his or her actions. Even here, and to be kind to the judge, perhaps this was what he was struggling to vocalise, matters are not clear cut. A person who crosses this boundary is not necessarily a "sex offender" or a "paedophile" except technically. It is certainly true that this powerful label, which denotes a person who pathologically views children as sexual objects, is bandied around rather too freely at present.

Second, it is crucial that the law expects similar standards from all adults, even when they are of a fairly similar age. All adults should consider themselves to be in "a position of trust and responsibility" over children, not just those who work with them, however precocious a child may appear.

Other professionals are not expected to conduct sexual liaisons with their clients, and nor should people in the teaching profession, whatever age their "clients" are.

As for people under 16, no one should be having sexual relations with them at all, whatever the excuses they may offer. No judge should think otherwise.

12

The Legal System Overprotects Some Teens and Overpunishes Others

Dahlia Lithwick

Dahlia Lithwick is a contributing editor for Newsweek *and a senior editor for* Slate.

The legal system shows prejudice when it comes to dealing with teenagers. The courts base their judgments on the "type" of teenager they are dealing with, rather than the crime that he or she has committed or the crime committed against them. For example, 465 young people were removed from a Texas ranch, many of these underage mothers, because the Child Protection Services felt they were in danger. However, the courts ultimately deemed them mature enough to make their own decisions because of their Christian upbringing. Conversely, a young boy is being held for throwing a grenade that killed a U.S. soldier during a firefight when he was fifteen. In both situations, these children are products of their environment and were taught these beliefs of either polygamy or war, from childhood. A child-soldier bill, which would call for young people to be tried as children instead of adults, has already passed in the Senate and is now being contemplated by the House of Representatives, thus making the line between capable adult or incapable child a little more clear. However, the inability of the courts and society in general to see teenagers as wholly innocent and impressionable or wholly volatile and out of control continues to mar that line.

Anyone who's ever been 15 knows that the question of when childhood ends and adulthood begins is complicated. At that age, one can veer between rational decision-making and delusions of fabulous self-importance about 30 times each day. That's why our legal system tries—not always successfully—to draw a nuanced, fact-based line between childhood and adulthood. It's why the age of consent in some jurisdictions is 14 while in others it's 18, even though teenagers everywhere really, really like sex.

And that's why the comparison between the 465 youngsters seized from a Texas polygamist ranch in April [2008] and a young Canadian man currently [June 2008] being tried at Guantánamo Bay is so illuminating. In both cases, when it came to treating children like adults and adults like children, the government was hopelessly confused. Considered side by side, the two cases reflect our troubling legal tendency to overprotect those teens we deem to be victims and overpunish those we consider violent.

The Religious, Conservative Child

The decision by Texas Child Protective Services to pluck hundreds of youngsters from the compound of the Yearning for Zion ranch was rooted in a fatally romantic vision of childhood. In April [2008], the state initiated a sweeping raid based on what may have been a fraudulent sex-abuse hot-line call, as well as the state's allegation that five young girls at the ranch had been sexually abused by older men. Last month two state appellate courts determined that the removal of hundreds of small children and married, consenting women was unwarranted. Although Child Protective Services had argued that the young people were in immediate danger as a consequence of the polygamists' dangerous beliefs, the courts disagreed on both counts. Many of those removed were not children—the age of consent in Texas is 17, and of the 31 girls initially removed as underage mothers, 15 were, in fact, adults and one was 27—nor were they in any immediate danger, and many were old enough to make their own legal decisions. Furthermore, even if those decisions were the product of religious brainwashing, the appeals courts would not characterize exposure to those ideas as abuse.

In the eyes of the Pentagon, a 15-year-old kid was a wholly autonomous adult.

The Texas authorities mistakenly believed that everyone it had grabbed on the ranch was a too-impressionable child. The Texas courts, on the other hand, credited those same children with a broad capacity to make autonomous legal decisions. Teenagers who are sober, conservative, religious and married don't quite match up with our streetwise notions of contemporary MTV adolescence. But, in the eyes of the Texas courts, that doesn't necessarily make them victims of abuse.

The Volatile Child Soldier

Now consider Omar Khadr, a 21-year-old Canadian who has been held at Guantánamo Bay for six years while awaiting trial for crimes he is accused of committing in Afghanistan at age 15. Khadr faces a life sentence for allegedly throwing a grenade in a fire fight, which resulted in the death of a U.S. soldier. Khadr's lawyers had sought to have the case against him dismissed because the Optional Protocol of the U.N. Convention on the Rights of the Child affords special protections to soldiers under 18, treating them as victims to be rehabilitated. But last month the military judge presiding over Khadr's tribunal denied that motion, and so Khadr will be tried as an adult, just as he's been incarcerated and interrogated as one. In the eyes of the Pentagon, a 15-year-old kid was a wholly autonomous adult.

The House is now contemplating a child-soldier bill, which has already passed in the Senate.[1] Like the U.N. Convention on the Rights of the Child, the legislation deems young soldiers under 18 as fundamentally different from adults, and one provision would seek to prosecute anyone involved in the "recruitment or training" of juveniles under the age of 15. Nobody disputes that Omar Khadr was radicalized by his father as early as age 11, when he was trotted around Afghanistan to meet with Al Qaeda big shots, so how can it be that Khadr is both the "victim" of recruitment and training and also a full-fledged, culpable adult? Like the Texas Child Protective Services system, the child-soldier bill assumes that children are enormously susceptible to brainwashing—so much so that their own decisions, even the choice to take up arms, are not free and autonomous. Like the youngsters at the Yearning for Zion ranch, Khadr is thus a child by one legal model and an adult by a second.

Are these teens innocent teenage victims or incorrigible demons?

So which one is it? Are these teens innocent teenage victims or incorrigible demons? Are they grown-ups with slightly less facial hair? Or the lapdogs of adults who brainwash them?

One way to reconcile the confused decisions about the Texas polygamists and Omar Khadr is to recognize that the legal system operates in broad caricatures when it comes to children, manifesting disproportionate fear of violent kids as wholly out of control while treating all victims as though they are incapable of protecting themselves. Maybe all this legal confusion is a function of the dual nature of American teenagers, who invariably seem too old and too young for their own good. Or maybe it just reflects our own larger uncer-

---

1. The Child Soldiers Accountability Act of 2008 was signed by George W. Bush on October 3, 2008.

tainty about whether to believe too broadly that teens are per-fect and pure—or dangerous, unguided missiles.

13

Sarah's Law Expands the Rights of Parents and Children

Anonymous

The author of this viewpoint is a staff writer for a conservative student publication.

California's Proposition 4, also known as Sarah's Law, would require parental notification before an abortion is performed on a minor in California. Many argue that the law is a violation of an individual's rights, but it actually supports the young pregnant woman's right to be able to make a clear, uncoerced decision, as well as to receive safe medical treatment should she decide on an abortion. The same people who argue against Proposition 4 because of legal costs in dealing with such cases, also admit that the decrease in cost of dealing with issues of sexually transmitted diseases and teen pregnancies would outweigh those concerns. Opponents also argue that the safety of girls will be at stake if they have abusive parents, but there is a provision in the law stating that another family member may be notified, instead of the parents, in such cases. Overall, Sarah's Law protects the rights of children as well as the rights of parents to know what their children are doing.

The penetrating voice of San Francisco's mayor, Gavin Newsom, could be heard projecting across Sproul Plaza last week. With great conviction he urged the students of UC Ber-

"Yes On Proposition 4: Protect Children and Support Families' Rights," *California Patriot*, November 1, 2008. Reproduced by permission.

keley to "get up and vote down Proposition 4". He then asked the audience why we should vote for Proposition 4, a measure that would require parental notification before an abortion is performed on a minor. After all, according to Mayor Newsom, it would be "the first amendment in the constitution that limits individuals' rights." Surely, Californians on both sides of the aisle are ultimately interested in decreasing the number of abortions and protecting the best interest of young pregnant women. So the important question is: how will this proposition affect the rights of pregnant minors and their safety?

Proposition 4, also known as Sarah's Law, would prohibit abortion for unemancipated minors until 48 hours after physician notifies the minor's parent, legal guardian, or if parental abuse has been reported, an alternative adult family member. There are several exceptions to the law designed to further protect the health and safety of pregnant minors. Proposition 4 provides exceptions for medical emergency or parental waiver, and would permit courts to waive notice based on clear and convincing evidence of minor's maturity or best interests. Additionally, it would permit judicial relief if the minor's consent is coerced, and furthermore, it would allow an adult relative of the minor seeking an abortion to be notified if the minor's parents are abusive (ballotpedia.org).

Parents have the right to know what their minor is doing, especially when it involves a potentially life threatening procedure.

Critics of this potential law cite increased costs as one of the reasons why this proposition is flawed. They claim that the annual costs to local law enforcement and courts would be in the range of $5 million to $6 million per year; however, the same critics do acknowledge that these costs could be partially or completely offset by a savings from the potential decrease in sexually transmitted diseases, teenage pregnancies. Another issue taken with the proposition is that it would endanger the safety of teenagers with abusive parents; the proposition would allegedly cause minors who fall into this category to suffer abuse or cause them to resort to a back-alley abortion out of fear. Essentially, those in opposition to Proposition 4 maintain that the proposition would not only diminish the rights of pregnant teenage girls but it would also endanger their health and safety.

Although Mayor Newsom and other opponents adamantly assert that Proposition 4 is an encroachment upon the rights and well-being of minors, they actually have it completely backwards. Proposition 4 would reclaim the rights of pregnant minors as well as their families and actually protect the health of both the mother and the baby. The safety of pregnant teenagers would be enhanced as they could fully consider the risks of a potentially life threatening abortion by discussing it with adults who are close to them. Ultimately, the choice should lie in the judgment of the pregnant minor and her family members, not the pressure from a Planned Parenthood employee, a doctor, or her peers.

Proposition 4 expands the rights of the parents as well. Parents have the right to know what their minor is doing, especially when it involves a potentially life threatening procedure. To highlight one of the possible complications of an abortion, the risk of breast cancer almost doubles if an abortion is performed on a first pregnancy during the first trimester of the pregnancy (www.allaboutpopularissues.org). There are far less dangerous activities for which minors need parental approval. Minors need parental consent to get their teeth cleaned at the dentist and even to use a tanning bed. If parents have the right to decide if a fake tan is unsafe for their daughter, they certainly have the right to decide if an abortion is too dangerous. Even those who do not view life as beginning with conception must see that the health of both the mother and child are protected by Proposition 4. Additionally, the accommodations for teenagers who have abusive parents ensure that every minor is protected from harm while still allowing for a parental figure to provide guidance and support in the decision making process.

And while nearly all of Mayor Newsom's comments last week were egregiously inaccurate, he did have one thing correct; Proposition 4 is about our rights. While the opponents of this proposition attempt to deceive the public through their guile and deceptive rhetoric, Proposition 4 will undoubtedly protect the precedence of a family's judgment in private matters, and most importantly protect the health of pregnant minors. So when in the voting booth, remember; Proposition 4 is an issue of rights, and Gavin Newsom is not interested in protecting yours.

Organizations to Contact

The editors have compiled the following list of organizations concerned with the issues debated in this book. The descriptions are derived from materials provided by the organizations. All have publications or information available for interested readers. The list was compiled on the date of publication of the present volume; the information provided here may change. Be aware that many organizations take several weeks or longer to respond to inquiries, so allow as much time as possible for the receipt of requested materials.

4Parents.gov
U.S. Department of Health and Human Services
Washington, DC   20201
(240) 453-2828
Web site: www.4parents.gov

A national public education campaign, 4Parents.gov makes available to parents information to help teenage children make informed decisions about sex. The Web site puts emphasis on the importance of a caring parent in the teen's life as well as encouraging abstinence until marriage.

Advocates for Youth
2000 M St. NW, Suite 750, Washington, DC   20036
(202) 419-3420 • fax: (202) 419-1448
Web site: www.advocatesforyouth.org

Advocates for Youth was founded in 1980 as the Center for Population Options. For nearly thirty years it has worked to promote better and more effective sexual health and education programs and policies, not only in the United States, but in other countries as well. Its mission is based on rights, respect, and responsibility. The organization offers numerous publications, including reports, lesson plans, and fact sheets, on its Web site.

Center for Law and Social Policy (CLASP)
1015 15th St. NW, Suite 400, Washington, DC   20005
(202) 906-8000 • fax: (202) 842-2885
Web site: www.clasp.org

CLASP focuses on helping low-income families and the disadvantaged, by improving the child support and welfare systems, as well as by supporting the integration of childcare and early education programs. Its Web site offers reports, fact sheets, and other materials, including many that focus on age of consent issues.

The Coalition for Positive Sexuality (CPS)
PO Box 77212, Washington, DC   20013
(773) 604-1654
Web site: www.positive.org

CPS began in 1996 as a poster project encouraging girls to acknowledge their sexuality, not deny it. The project also offers useful information about safe sex and sexually transmitted diseases. It's current publication *Just Say Yes* can be obtained by visiting the Web site.

Community Alliance for the Ethical Treatment of Youth (CAFETY)
277 Starr St., 2nd Fl., Brooklyn, NY   11237
(877) 322-3389
Web site: www.cafety.org

CAFETY is committed to the protection of the human rights of young people who have emotional, mental, and behavioral disabilities. Its current "Care, Not Coercion" program aims to increase awareness of youth programs and bring attention to states that allow practices detrimental to youth due to inadequate regulatory policy or ineffective monitoring. The organization's Web site offers a wealth of information on current laws and policies as well as opportunities to get involved in its campaign.

Mobilization of America's Youth (MAY)

2105 Martin Luther King Way, 2nd Fl., Berkeley, CA   94704
(510) 717-3022
e-mail: info@mobilize.org
Web site: www.mobilize.org

MAY was created in 2002 by members and activists of the student government at the University of California-Berkeley. Its goal is to educate and empower young people to increase their political participation, informing them of the ways in which public policy affects them and how they may affect public policy. Its Web site includes a discussion of age of consent issues.

My 5th

621 North Ave. NE, Bldg. B, Atlanta, GA   30308
(404) 522-1200 • fax: (404) 810-9092
e-mail: my5th.org@gmail.org
Web site: www.my5th.org

My 5th was founded by BJ Bernstein, an Atlanta-based criminal defense lawyer. The Web site, based on the premise that ignorance of the law is no excuse, uses comprehensive videos to help young people understand the laws that could possibly send them to jail. In addition to the videos, the Web site features a blog that discusses current events related to youth and the law.

The National Campaign to Prevent Teen and Unplanned Pregnancy

1776 Massachusetts Ave. NW, Suite 200
Washington, DC   20036
(202) 478-8500 • fax: (202) 478-8588
Web site: www.thenationalcampaign.org

The National Campaign to Prevent Teen and Unplanned Pregnancy was formed in 1996 in an effort to decrease teen pregnancy in America. The organization works with policy makers, the media, and state and local leaders, to provide materials needed to educate parents, teens, and young adults on the prevention of teen pregnancy. The organization also works directly with teens through its Youth On-Line Network.

Queer Youth Network

c/o Lesbian and Gay Centre, Manchester   M1 7HB
   United Kingdom
0870-383-4796 • fax: +44-161-241-6733
e-mail: info@queeryouth.net
Web site: www.queeryouth.org.uk

David Joseph Henry and Charlotte Lester founded the Queer Youth Network in 1999 as a civil rights group. The organization focus on youth support and the prevention of homophobic legislation. It is currently fighting for same-sex marriage and an equal age of consent for homosexuals.

ReformSexOffenderLaws.Org

c/o Indochina Newsletter, Cambridge, MA   02140
(800) 773-43219
e-mail: info@ReformSexOffenderLaws.org
Web site: www.reformsexoffenderlaws.org

ReformSexOffenderLaws.Org was founded in the late 1990s by a group of civil libertarians, educators, and other professionals who were concerned about the unjust laws created as a result of public panic about sex between minors. Its main goal, through supporting and creating programs for children and youth, is to empower young people to make informed decisions about their lives. The organization's Web site includes relevant reports and links to related research as well as a bibliography of discussion materials.

Youth Incentives

PO Box 9022, Utrecht   3506 GA
   The Netherlands
+31-(0)30-2332322 • fax: +31-(0)30-2319387
e-mail: info@youthincentives.org
Web site: www.youthincentives.org

Youth Incentives, part of the International Programme on Sexuality, was developed by the Rutgers Nisso Group, an expert center on sexuality, located in the Netherlands. Its approach to lowering teen pregnancy and sexually transmitted diseases is through education and openness about the sexuality of youth. Its publications, including *Educational Programmes for Sex Offenders* and *Juvenile Sex Offenders Need Guidance*, may be downloaded for free from the organization's Web site.

Bibliography

Books

Bill Ameiss   *Love, Sex, and God: For Young Men Ages 15 and Up*. St. Louis, MO: Concordia Publishing House, 2008.

Richard Bimler   *Sex and the New You: For Young Women Ages 13–15*. St. Louis, MO: Concordia Publishing House, 2008.

Carolyn Cocca   *Jailbait: The Politics of Statutory Rape Laws in the United States*. Albany, NY: State University of New York, 2004.

Heather Corinna   *S.E.X.: The All-You-Need-To-Know Progressive Sexuality Guide to Get You Through High School and College*. New York: De Capo Press, 2007.

J. Shoshanna Ehrlich   *Who Decides?: The Abortion Rights of Teens*. Santa Barbara, CA: Praeger, 2006.

Richard B. Gartner   *Beyond Betrayal: Taking Charge of Your Life After Boyhood Sexual Abuse*. New York: Wiley, 2005.

Rebecca Probert   *Responsible Parents and Parental Responsibility*. Oxford, United Kingdom: Hart Publishing, 2009.

Tina Radziszewicz *Ready or Not?: A Girl's Guide to Making Her Own Decisions About Dating, Love and Sex.* New York: Walker and Company, 2006.

Jaya Sagade *Child Marriage in India: Socio-Legal and Human Rights Dimensions.* Oxford, United Kingdom: Oxford University Press, 2005.

Matthew Waites *The Age of Consent: Young People, Sexuality and Citizenship.* New York: Palgrave MacMillan, 2009.

Periodicals

Augusta Chronicle "Loophole Awaits Legislation," June 17, 2009.

Catholic Insight "Raising the Age of Consent," July 30, 2005.

Dean Cook "Age of Consent Laws," DeanCook.net, March 8, 2008.

Shaunti Feldhahn and Andrea Cornell Sarvady "Should 'Sexting' Be Decriminalized?" *The Atlanta Journal Constitution*, April 24, 2009.

Kaj Hasselriis "Should the Age of Consent Be Raised? A Conservative Bill Proposing That the Age of Sexual Consent Be Raised Has Feminists Divided," *Herizons*, March 22, 2007.

The Independent "Common Sense about the Age of Consent," November 20, 2006.

Irish Independent	"Debate On Age of Consent Misses the Point," December 13, 2006.
Jeff Israely	"Berlusconi and the Girl: No Spice, Thank You," *Time*, May 29, 2009.
Dan Izenberg	"You're 17? Wait 'til You're 18!" *The Jerusalem Post*, November 16, 2007.
Miles O'Brien	"The Age of Consent," *The Gleaner*, January 14, 2004.
Donna O'Neil	"Inappropriate Coach—He Didn't Know Relationship with Student Was Wrong," *The Wakefield Observer*, March 16, 2009.
Tony Perkins	"Kevin Jennings—Unsafe for America's Schools," Human Events.com, June 29, 2009.
Wayne Allyn Root	"Anarchism, Age of Consent Laws and the Dallas Accord," crazyforliberty.com, May 7, 2008.
Nate Silver	"Pro-Life States Have Lower Abortion Rates," *FiveThirtyEight*, June 2, 2009.
Teacherrowie. blogspot.com	"The Age of Consent," December 6, 2006.
Sarah Womack	""Drop Age of Consent to 14, Says Academic," *Telegraph.co.uk*, February 2007.

Index

A

Abortion laws, 12, 21, 77–80
Abortion rates, 10–11
Abstinence, 28, 29
ACLU (American Civil Liberties Union), 38
The Adam Walsh Act, 59
Adolescents
    abortion rights, 77–80
    eroticism, 32–36
    life stage, 26–28, 61, 63
    sex offender registration by, 46–47, 49–50, 52
    viewpoints, 29–30
    See also Behavior, adolescent; Puberty; Sexual activity, adolescent
Adult-child relationships. *See* Relationships, adult-child
Age
    adult-child relationships, 10–12
    competence, 16–18
    entering puberty, 15–16, 21
    legal homosexuality, 29
Age of consent laws
    criminalizing normal behavior, 46–52
    gender-biased enforcement, 50, 67–71
    history, 15, 26, 48–49
    inconsistencies, 26–27, 29
    marriage, 8, 11–12
    maturity levels, 21–22, 73–76
    See also Prosecution; Statutory rape laws
AIDS, 11

American Civil Liberties Union (ACLU), 38
Australian law, 26–29

B

Barry, Jody, 64
Behavior, adolescent
    adult-child relationships, 32–36, 51
    fair assessment, 73–76
    influence of law, 11–12
    maturity, 16–18, 22–23, 28
    See also Sexting; Sexual activity, adolescent
Beyond Borders, 56
Birth control, 21
Boundaries, personal, 20–21, 22–24
Bozell, Brent, 37–40
Brainwashing, 74, 75
British law, 21

C

To Catch a Predator (show), 51
Child abuse
    abortion laws, 78–80
    adult influence, 73–74
    homosexuality, 56–57, 69
    See also Relationships, adult-child
Child Protective Services, Texas, 73–74
Children's health
    age of puberty onset, 15–16, 21

89